Shire County Guide 19

KENT

John E. Vigar

Shire Publications Ltd

Published in 1997 by Shire Publications Ltd, Cromwell House, Church Street, Princes Risborough, Buckinghamshire HP27 9AA, UK.

Printed in Great Britain by CIT Printing Services, Press Buildings, Merlins Bridge, Haverfordwest, Pembrokeshire SA61 1XF.

British Library Cataloguing in Publication Data: Vigar, John E. Kent. – 3rd ed. – (Shire county guide; 19) 1. Kent (England) – Guidebooks I. Title 914.2'23'04859 ISBN 0-7478-0335-8

Acknowledgements

Photographs are acknowledged as follows: Colin Bourner, pages 60 and 64; English Heritage, pages 50, 51 and 54; the Faversham Society, pages 85 and 97; Dorothy Leavers, page 107; Maidstone Museum and Art Gallery (Ronald White), pages 87 and 90; Sloman & Petit, page 55; John E. Vigar, page 26. The remaining photographs, including the cover, are by Cadbury Lamb. The street plans on pages 13 and 28 are by D. R. Darton. The map on pages 4 and 5 is by Robert Dizon, using Ordnance Survey Material. The National Grid References in the text are included by permission of the Controller of Her Majesty's Stationery Office.

Ordnance Survey grid references

Although information on how to reach most of the places described in this book by car is given in the text, National Grid References are also included in many instances, particularly for the harder-to-find places in chapters 3, 4 and 9, for the benefit of those readers who have the Ordnance Survey 1:50,000 Landranger maps of the area. The references are stated as a Landranger sheet number followed by the 100 km National Grid square and the six-figure reference.

To locate a site by means of the grid reference, proceed as in the following example: Chillenden Windmill (OS 179: TR 269543). Take the OS Landranger map sheet 179 ('Canterbury and East Kent'). The grid numbers are printed in blue around the edges of the map. In more recently produced maps these numbers are repeated at 10 km intervals throughout the map, so that it is not necessary to open it out completely.) Read off these numbers from the left along the top edge of the map until you come to 26, denoting a vertical grid line, then estimate nine-tenths of the distance to vertical line 27 and envisage an imaginary vertical grid line 26.9 at this point. Next look at the grid numbers at one side of the map (either side will do) and read *upwards* until you find the horizontal grid line 54. Estimate three-tenths of the distance to the next horizontal line above (i.e. 55), and so envisage an imaginary horizontal line across the map at 54.3. Follow this imaginary line across the map until it crosses the imaginary vertical line 26.9. At the intersection of these two lines you will find Chillenden Windmill.

The Ordnance Survey Landranger maps which cover Kent are sheets 177, 178, 179, 188 and 189. Small areas of the county are found on maps 187 and 199.

Cover: *The picturesque village street at Chiddingstone, a property of the National Trust.*

Contents

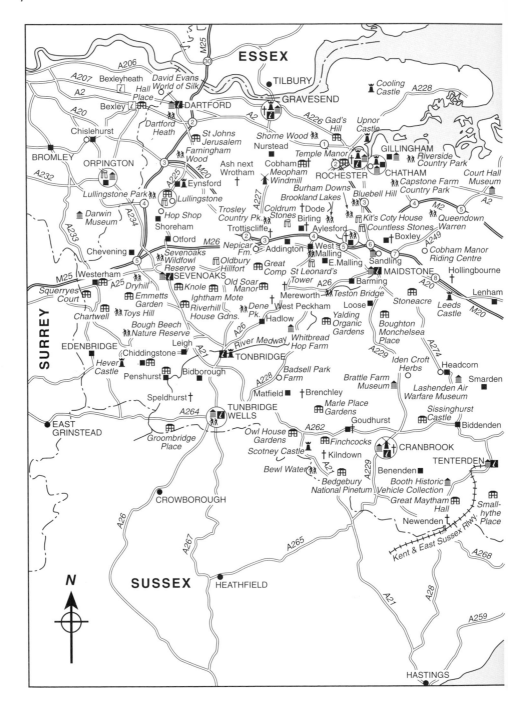

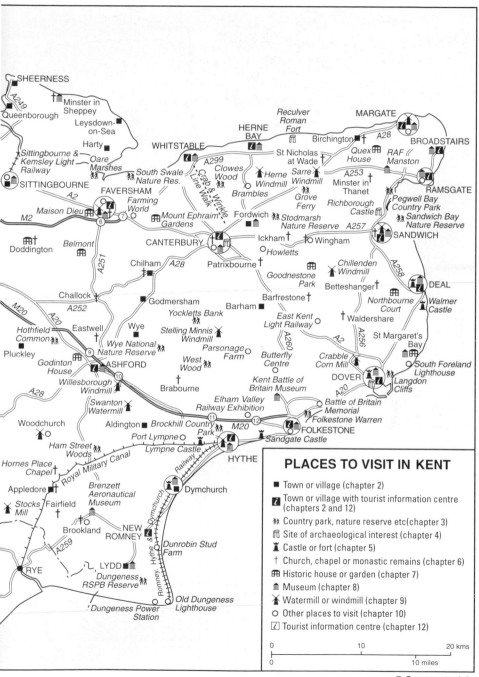

PLACES TO VISIT IN KENT

- ■ Town or village (chapter 2)
- *i* Town or village with tourist information centre (chapters 2 and 12)
- ✺ Country park, nature reserve etc(chapter 3)
- ⋔ Site of archaeological interest (chapter 4)
- ♟ Castle or fort (chapter 5)
- † Church, chapel or monastic remains (chapter 6)
- ⊞ Historic house or garden (chapter 7)
- ⏛ Museum (chapter 8)
- ✱ Watermill or windmill (chapter 9)
- O Other places to visit (chapter 10)
- *i* Tourist information centre (chapter 12)

0   10   20 kms

0   10 miles

© Crown copyright

Preface

Welcome to the Shire County Guide to Kent, one of over thirty such books, written and designed to enable you to organise your time in the county well.

The Shire County Guides fill the need for a compact, accurate and thorough guide to each county so that visitors can plan a half-day excursion or a whole week's stay to best advantage. Residents, too, will find the guides a handy and reliable reference to the places of interest in their area.

Travelling British roads can be time consuming, and the County Guides will ensure that you need not inadvertently miss any interesting feature in a locality, that you do not accidentally bypass a new museum or an outstanding church, that you can find an attractive place to picnic, and that you will appreciate the history and the buildings of the towns or villages in which you stop.

This book has been arranged in special interest chapters, such as the countryside, historic houses or archaeological sites, and all these places of interest are located on the map on pages 4-5. Use the map either for an overview to decide which area has most to interest you, or to help you enjoy your immediate neighbourhood. Then refer to the nearest town or village in chapter 2 to see, at a glance, what special features or attractions each community contains or is near. The subsequent chapters enable readers with a particular interest to find immediately those places of importance to them, while the cross-referencing under 'Kent towns and villages' assists readers with wider tastes to select how best to spend their time.

The Calico House in Newnham village.

1
The Garden of England

From earliest times Kent has been one of the more important counties in England, owing to its proximity to the continent. This geographical location has had both positive and negative effects on the development of the county. New ideas and wealth have reached Kent before other parts of England but at the same time invasions have had more of an impact on the county and its people than on most other areas.

The geology of Kent has made it a county of contrasts. The fertile valleys of the rivers Medway and Stour give way to the North Downs, an enormous chalk escarpment. These in turn are bordered by tidal marshes to the north and the English Channel to the east. Because of the chalk Kent became an industrial area during the middle ages. The Romans, who landed in Pegwell Bay, used chalk for agricultural purposes, but the widespread building programme of the Normans brought its use to the fore, not as building stone but as an ingredient of mortar and rendering. The continued use of chalk has left deep scarring on the countryside, especially in the north.

Yet it is as the 'Garden of England' that Kent is best-known. Although much agricultural land is now under the plough or used for grazing, areas of orchards and hop gardens, with their associated oast houses, are still to be found.

In the east the white cliffs of Dover have been the last view of England for many a traveller and a welcome sight to those returning from afar.

Kent has suffered not only from its proximity to the continent but also for its position close to London, which over the past two hundred years has become an unwelcome neighbour. As soon as London developed people began to use Kent as a convenient corridor, and advances in transport have made this even more true today. If more people would stop to discover the delights hidden off the beaten track they would realise that Kent has a great deal to offer.

Residents of the county are frequently asked to which group they belong – Men of Kent or Kentish Men, for traditionally those born in the county are categorised according to which side of the river Medway they were born. The modern controversy was started by Shakespeare in *King Henry VI*, although the river had been an early boundary as early as AD 455 when the Jutish invaders Hengist and Horsa fought the king of Kent, Vortigern, at Aylesford. For the first time in the history of the British Isles there was a single army fighting for the national cause and for this reason the battle of Aylesford is referred to as 'the place where England began'. The county emblem, a white horse on a red shield, was first used by Hengist and Horsa at this battle, in which the local tribes were defeated. Today the emblem may be found on all official documents and in many other applications, giving the county a sense of pride and a feeling of independence.

The south-western portion of the county forms the Weald, a low fertile area that represents rural Kent at its best. Thousands of years ago this formed the highest land in southern England, made up of a huge dome of chalk. Over the years this eroded away to leave the North Downs in Kent and the South Downs in Sussex as the rim of a large saucer-like hollow. This area, protected by the high edges and blessed with abundant water supplies, became a dense forest that provided much timber during the medieval period. This was not only used locally to build countless houses and churches but was also employed elsewhere in shipbuilding and construction. Even today large areas of the county are enforested, although much of this woodland is commercially managed.

Throughout history Kent has been radical in its outlook. Rebellions, both local and national, have frequently flared up – partly because of the diverse cultures represented in its population. Wat Tyler encouraged the Peasant's Revolt to start at Maidstone in 1381. Two hundred years later the marriage of Queen Mary to Philip of Spain prompted the Protestant landowners of Kent to rebel, although they were soon quashed. During the Civil War Kent saw many skirmishes, the most notable being the battle of Maidstone in 1648.

The Kent coastline was important throughout the middle ages, as four of the original Cinque Ports were established there. Cross-channel traffic and the need to counter attacks from England's enemies created wealth and a certain amount of stability along the coast. In times of peace it was much easier to get from London to the Channel ports of Sandwich and Dover by boat rather than to travel overland, and so feeder towns became an important part of the north Kent landscape, the best-known examples being Gravesend and Faversham.

In the eighteenth century the Isle of Thanet began to develop as a tourist resort, the small fishing villages growing and adapting to cater for the large numbers of visitors who came to swim and drink the sea water. Terraces of elegant houses were built and let 'for the season'. Other coastal towns, further from London around the coast, did not develop until the arrival of the railway in the mid nineteenth century made them easily accessible from the capital.

The world's first passenger railway was opened in Kent in 1830. It ran between Canterbury and Whitstable, a distance of about 6 miles (10 km) and its aim was to link Canterbury with the Thames for commercial benefit. Its engineers were Robert and George Stephenson and the *Invicta* steam engine may still be seen at Canterbury Heritage (see page 80). The line, however, was not a success as at 9d each way the fare was too expensive.

More than any other period it was the nineteenth century that changed the face of Kent. Villages were established to serve areas of new industry and enlarged agricultural estates. Towns were deliberately expanded with large villas and formal drives. Pride in the county and in individual towns manifested itself in a plethora of town halls, clock-towers and public libraries, whilst hardly a village was left without a new hall or chapel. Kent had become the prosperous middle-class stronghold that it remains to this day.

No longer was the county dependent on the land. Railways and improved roads, the growth of local industries and the move from manual to clerical employment had changed the face of Kent forever. Everyone looked forward with renewed enthusiasm and the past was pushed firmly into the background. This has left the present-day visitor with a feeling that Kent has little to offer. The county certainly hides its treasures well, but with a growing awareness of heritage and conservation issues more and more people are coming to discover that Kent has a tremendous wealth of history, on which the modern successes have been built.

Appledore village.

2
Kent towns and villages

Addington

A peaceful backwater near West Malling, Addington is typical of the villages that grew in the middle ages as a result of being granted a market charter. The market lasted only a few years, but the result is that the village has a charming green overlooked by a fifteenth-century inn. Just outside the village centre are the remains of two small neolithic burial chambers which may be visited on application.

In the locality: Coldrum Stones, page 49; Nepicar Farm, page 102; church at Trottiscliffe, page 68.

Aldington

The village is famous as the base for a notorious gang of smugglers in the early nineteenth century. The Aldington Gang was the best-known of several organised groups who exploited the sparsely populated areas of Romney Marsh. Aldington was a possession of the Archbishops of Canterbury and the magnificence of its church reflects the wealth of the area in the middle ages. It was the birthplace of Elizabeth Barton, the Holy Maid of Kent (see page 108).

In the locality: Lympne Castle, page 56; Port Lympne Wild Animal Park, page 104; Swanton Watermill, page 99.

Appledore

Although there is little more than one street to Appledore it is a delightful village to come across after driving across the open marshland. It was first mentioned in the Anglo-Saxon Chronicle as the scene of one of the many Danish invasions of the ninth century. Five hundred years later it suffered a French invasion, when many of the buildings were destroyed or damaged. Another five hundred years later, during the Napoleonic Wars, there was again the threat of a French invasion and the Royal Military Canal was con-structed as a defence. There are some delightful houses along the green verges, and the church contains many items of interest. Outside the village is the delightful ancient monument of Hornes Place Chapel.

Church of St Peter and St Paul, page 59; **Hornes Place Chapel**, page 65.

Ashford

Early closing Wednesday; street markets Tuesday and Friday, general market Saturday.

Today Ashford is firmly on the map of Britain, with its International station rising like a spaceship above the nineteenth-century houses of this Victorian railway town. It was the railway, with lines radiating to Tonbridge, Maidstone, Canterbury, Folkestone and Hastings, that transformed a small market town into a major engineering centre. Ashford is also a commercial centre for the small agricultural estates with which this part of Kent is dotted. The pedestrianised centre of the town is picturesque, relieved by a locally infamous ring road. There are few individual buildings of note in the town, but the parish church contains many interesting memorials, including one to John Fogge, who paid for the church to be rebuilt in the fifteenth century.

Ashford Borough Museum, page 79.

In the locality: Godinton House, page 71; South of England Rare Breeds Centre, page 105; Swanton Watermill, page 99; Willesborough Windmill, page 99.

Ash next Wrotham

Church of St Peter and St Paul, page 00.

Aylesford

This is the place where England began. The battle of Aylesford, which took place in AD 455 between the tribes of Britain and the Jutish invaders Hengist and Horsa, resulted in the formation of the English nation. In the middle ages this picturesque village became a small market town, helped by the foundation of a priory nearby. Although the picture postcard view of Aylesford is well-known, there are many other pretty corners to be discovered. Guided tours of the village for groups may be arranged by telephoning 01622 718118. Outside the village the Countless Stones and Kit's Coty House may be seen and there are fine views across the Medway valley from Bluebell Hill.

Aylesford Priory, page 59; **Countless Stones,** page 49; **Kit's Coty House,** page 49.

In the locality: Museum of Kent Life, page 90; Tyland Barn, page 105.

Barfrestone

Church of St Nicholas, page 60.

Barham

Barham is a sleepy village lying in a fold of the Downs. The copper-spired church has much of interest, including the war memorial which bears the name of Lord Kitchener of Khartoum, who lived at Broome Park, a seventeenth-century mansion that is now a country club. Much of the land around here was occupied by the army during the Second World War and in the church there is a good twentieth-century window, designed by Martin Travers, which commemorates the signallers who were stationed here.

In the locality: Howletts Wild Animal Park, page 102; Stelling Minnis Windmill, page 99; church at Patrixbourne, page 66.

Barming

The river Medway narrows here, with the land dropping steeply to a little wooden bridge overlooked by orchards and hop gardens. Fine walks may be taken along the river at this point, the path sandwiched between the riverbank and railway line. There is no real village centre, the church being isolated in fields. This discourages visitors, but there is much of note, including some exceptional Flemish carving in the choir stalls.

In the locality: Boughton Monchelsea Place, page 69; St Leonard's Tower, page 52; Yalding Organic Gardens, page 78; church at Mereworth, page 65.

Bekesbourne

Howletts Wild Animal Park, page 102.

Benenden

One of the largest village greens in Kent is surrounded by a mixture of delightful medieval houses, the impressive parish church and many estate houses built by the Earl of Cranbook in the nineteenth century. Lord Cranbrook's enormous mansion, originally called Hemsted, now houses the famous Benenden School, and the whole area is impeccably maintained. The gardens of nearby Hole Park are occasionally open to the public.

Betteshanger

Church of St Mary, page 60.

Bexley

Hall Place, page 72.

Bidborough

One of the glories of Kent is Bidborough Ridge, along which the by-road from Tonbridge to Penshurst runs. The best time to drive along here is early evening, when the setting sun lights up the vast expanse of the upper Medway valley. The views were exploited in the 1920s and 1930s when large houses were built along the ridge, away from the old village centre. The church is worth a visit, if only to see the stained glass designed by Edward Burne-Jones and made by Morris and Company, and visitors will also notice the clock pendulum which swings beneath the tower.

In the locality: Badsell Park Farm, page 100; Penshurst Place, page 76; Penshurst Vineyard, page 105; Tonbridge Castle, page 57; and church at Speldhurst, page 68.

Biddenden

On the green are effigies of the Biddenden Maids, Siamese twins born in about 1100. They were joined at the waist and shoulders. On their deaths they left land in the village to provide bread and cheese for poor residents. This tradition is still maintained each Easter, when hard 'biscuits' bearing a picture of the maids are distributed. In the fifteenth century the village was the home of weavers, who had

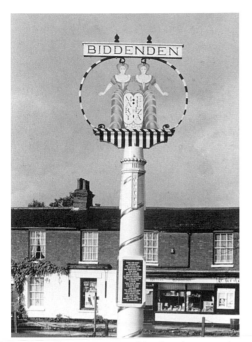

The village sign at Biddenden features the famous Siamese twins, the Biddenden Maids.

come here after persecution on the continent. They worked in first-floor rooms lit by large windows, which may still be seen. The church has a good set of memorial brasses dating from the fourteenth to sixteenth centuries.

Biddenden Vineyards, page 105.

In the locality: Kent & East Sussex Railway, page 102; Sissinghurst Castle Garden, page 77; Tenterden and District Museum, page 94.

Birchington

A large village on the main Thanet road, Birchington was originally a market town. In the nineteenth century it spread towards the sea and the architecture reveals much about the periods of expansion. The heart of the medieval village is dominated by the church, where the artist Dante Gabriel Rossetti is buried (see page 109), and there are several smugglers' cottages. The grand house in Quex Park stands a little way to the east, whilst to the west are large areas of open grassland and clifftop walks.

Church of All Saints, page 60; **Quex House**, page 76.

In the locality: Draper's Mill, page 98; Minster Abbey, page 66; Reculver Roman Fort, page 50; church at St Nicholas at Wade, page 67.

Birling

Birling is an estate village, recreated by the Neville family in the nineteenth century. The family has been associated with the village for eight hundred years, although their nineteenth-century mansion has been demolished. The picturesque village centre is dominated by two buildings, the parish church and the village forge. The former contains many reminders of the Nevilles, including the remarkable cast-iron door to the Neville family vault, and a tall font cover carved by three sisters in the nineteenth century. The village forge is still in operation. Opposite is a horse-chestnut tree, a reminder that the song 'Under the Spreading Chestnut Tree' was written in the village at the beginning of the twentieth century.

Church of All Saints, page 60.

In the locality: Coldrum Stones, page 49; New College of Cobham, page 75; Owletts, page 76; St Leonard's Tower, page 52; church at Dode, page 64.

Boughton Monchelsea

Boughton Monchelsea Place, page 69.

Boxley

Boxley is the quintessential English village, with manor house, church and inn surrounding a village green. Several famous people from English history have been associated with the village, the most notable being Alfred, Lord Tennyson, who took a house here during his sister's engagement to Edmund Lushington, who lived at Sandling Park. It is suggested that Tennyson's poem 'The Brook' was based on the countryside hereabouts. Outside the village is Boxley Abbey, a Cistercian monastery now converted to a mansion house (not open to the public). Its magnificent tithe barn may catch the eye from the M20 at junction 6.

Church of St Mary and All Saints, page 61.

In the locality: Aylesford Priory, page 59; Kit's Coty House, page 49; Museum of Kent Life, page 90; Stoneacre, page 78; Tyland Barn, page 105.

Brabourne
Church of St Mary, page 61.

Brenchley
Church of All Saints, page 61; Marle Place Gardens, page 75.

Brenzett
Aeronautical Museum, page 79.

Broadstairs
Early closing Wednesday.
This is the least spoilt Kent seaside town. The tall cliffs lead down to the tiny harbour which bustles with pleasure craft and fishing boats. On the hill above are Bleak House and the Dickens House Museum. A Dickens Festival is held each summer and the town has won awards in the Britain in Bloom competition. The original village settlement of St Peters, a couple of miles inland, has a picturesque centre with some fine examples of domestic architecture. On set days throughout the year residents dress up as characters associated with the history of the village and visitors can go on conducted tours to meet them. Advance booking is essential.

Bleak House Museum, page 79; **Crampton Tower Museum**, page 79; **Dickens House Museum**, page 80.

In the locality: Draper's Mill, page 98; Minster Abbey, page 66; Quex House, page 76; Shell Grotto, page 104.

Bromley
Early closing Wednesday.
Although the town has succumbed to the expansion of London, it remains an excellent shopping centre with good rail connections for those who live in Kent and want top-quality shopping without having to travel to London. The comfortable Churchill Theatre is also a great draw, offering excellent shows. A walk along the High Street reveals that the town was virtually rebuilt in the nineteenth century after the arrival of the railway. The buildings above the shop fronts show their original uses, often with the names of the first shops incorporated into the brickwork. The parish church suffered severe damage in the Second World War and little original work

survives. The author H. G. Wells was born in the High Street, where he is commemorated by a large mural. In recent years a major shopping and leisure complex has ensured that Bromley retains its position as an important regional centre.

In the locality: Bromley Museum, page 91; Chislehurst Caves, page 100; Crofton Roman Villa, page 49; Darwin Museum, page 85.

Brookland
Church of St Augustine, page 61, Philippine Village Craft Centre, page 104.

Canterbury
Early closing Thursday; market day Wednesday.
A perambulation of this historic city taking in most of the ancient buildings takes several hours. Park in one of the car parks in Watling Street or Castle Street. Watling Street was one of the main medieval streets, forming part of a grid plan. As one walks west the impression is of buildings constructed on a small scale. Near the junction with Castle Street, on the left, is a good example of eighteenth-century 'mathematical tiles' being used to conceal an earlier timber-framed building. These tiles were popular as an insulator and to bring a building up to date. At the end of Watling Street is the **Poor Priests' Hospital**, a medieval flint building founded in about 1200 and now housing a museum, Canterbury Heritage. Behind it, and reached under an archway, is the **Greyfriars**. Easily missed, this delightful building stands astride the river Stour. Just along East Street is another building built over the river, **Eastbridge Hospital**. This was founded to accommodate poor pilgrims during their stay in the city. Its refectory and undercroft are open to the public, although the rest of the building is an almshouse. Almost opposite Eastbridge Hospital is **The Weavers**, a fine row of timber-framed houses built to accommodate Flemish weavers in 1485. Not far away is the **Marlowe Theatre**, converted from the former Odeon cinema. It takes its name from Canterbury's famous playwright, Christopher Marlowe (see page 106). Closing the view down St Peter's Street are the **Westgate Towers**, the only

CANTERBURY

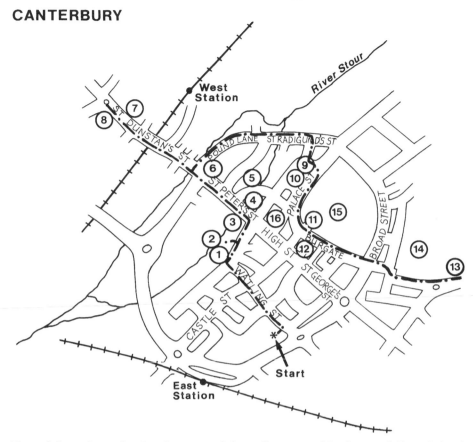

Plan of Canterbury, showing the route of the walk suggested in the text. 1 Poor Priests' Hospital. 2 Greyfriars. 3 Eastbridge Hospital. 4 The Weavers. 5 Marlowe Theatre. 6 Westgate Towers. 7 Roper Gateway. 8 St Dunstan's church. 9 King's School Shop. 10 Conquest House. 11 Christchurch Gateway. 12 Roman Museum. 13 St Martin's church. 14 St Augustine's Abbey. 15 Cathedral. 16 Royal Museum and Art Gallery.

surviving stone gateway in the city walls. It is built of ragstone and contains a museum.

On the far side of the gate, in St Dunstan's Street, are three interesting buildings. One is the **House of Agnes**, described by Charles Dickens as the home of Agnes Wickfield in *David Copperfield*. Further up the street is the **Roper Gateway**, all that remains of the house of the Roper family. Margaret Roper was the daughter of Sir Thomas More. When he was beheaded she retrieved his head from a pole on London Bridge and kept it in this house. After her death it was buried in the Roper Chapel in **St Dunstan's church** opposite.

The church draws thousands of visitors, not only for its associations with More, but because it is the only church in the city to be dedicated to St Dunstan, who was Archbishop of Canterbury from 959 to 988 and was England's most popular saint until the death of Becket.

Return through the Westgate Towers; the turning on the left, Pound Lane, leads into **St Radigund's Street**, which has an interesting selection of domestic architecture. **Palace Street** is the best-preserved street in the city. At the corner is the **King's School Shop**, with an eccentrically warped doorway. It

The Norman staircase at King's School, Canterbury.

was formerly the home of an Elizabethan lawyer. On the same side of the street is **Conquest House**, an interesting timber-framed structure. The **church of St Alphege** is now an exhibition centre. Palace Street runs into Burgate, where the **Buttermarket** forms a delightful square dominated by the **Christchurch Gateway** into the cathedral precincts. Under the new shopping centre is the **Roman Museum**. On the right-hand side of the road is the medieval tower of **St Mary's church**, demolished in 1871. It contains a magnificent seventeenth-century marble monument. Burgate ends at Broad Street, which should be crossed to visit **St Augustine's Abbey** and the outstanding **church of St Martin**.

    Canterbury Cathedral, page 61; **Canterbury Heritage**, page 80; **Canterbury Tales**, page 80; **church of St Martin**, page 63; **Great Stour Brewery**, page 101; **Roman Museum**, page 51; **Royal Museum and Art Gallery**, page 80; **St Augustine's**

Abbey, page 62; **Westgate Museum**, page 82.

    In the locality: Fordwich Town Hall, page 85; Howletts Wild Animal Park, page 102; church at Patrixbourne, page 66.

Challock

Church of St Cosmas and St Damian, page 63.

Chatham

Early closing Wednesday.
Chatham has a notable history and there is much of interest if one knows where to look. The High Street, which is now pedestrianised, offers a display of predictable shops, but there are some modern sculptures, and the historic Theatre Royal with its eastern influence gives some character to the western end of the precinct. On the boundary with Rochester stands Sir John Hawkins Hospital, built around a tiny square, with railings to the road. Opposite is Gundulf's Chapel, built in about 1140 and now overshadowed by new buildings. Below the railway station is a statue of Lieutenant Waghorn, who pioneered the overland route to India in the nineteenth century. St Mary's church, overlooking the river, has become a heritage centre charting the development of the area. Also in the town is a nineteenth-century pumping station. Excellent views over the town and river may be obtained by climbing on to the Great Lines, a huge military training area above the rooftops. Access may be obtained from the car park behind the Arts Centre in the former town hall.

    Chatham Historic Dockyard, page 82; **Fort Amherst**, page 54; **Medway Heritage Centre**, page 82; **Old Brook Pumping Station**, page 103; **Paddle Steamer** *Kingswear Castle*, page 86; **Theatre Royal**, page 105.

    In the locality: Capstone Farm Country Park, page 38; Kit's Coty House, page 49; Rochester Castle, page 56; Rochester Cathedral, page 67; Royal Engineers Museum, page 86; Upnor Castle, page 58; Temple Manor, page 78.

Chevening

Lying at the foot of the North Downs near

Sevenoaks, Chevening consists of a single street, church and mansion house. The mansion was built in the early seventeenth century and may be seen from the North Downs Way. It is now in the gift of the Prime Minister and is traditionally the weekend retreat of a minister of state. The gardens are occasionally opened for charitable causes. The church of St Botolph contains superb memorials to the Stanhope family, who lived at Chevening Park from the eighteenth century to the twentieth.

Chiddingstone

This unspoilt village is best-known for its main street, now owned by the National Trust. It is often used as a period setting for feature films. At the end of the street are the wrought-iron gates of Chiddingstone Castle. Originally the street ran through the park, but it was diverted in the late eighteenth century to give greater privacy to the castle. In the peaceful churchyard is the mausoleum of the Streatfeilds, who owned the castle. Their vault beneath contains over sixty coffins and is ventilated by an ingenious false altar tomb in the churchyard a few feet away. Just outside the village is the 'Chiding Stone', a natural sandstone outcrop that has come to be associated with the name of the village.

Chiddingstone Castle, page 70.

In the locality: Bough Beech Nature Reserve, page 35; Hever Castle, page 55; Penshurst Place, page 76; church at Speldhurst, page 68.

Chilham

A delightful village, Chilham is built around a market square between the church and castle. Although the church was much rebuilt in the nineteenth century it is well worth a visit. The North Downs Way runs through the village and one can often see walkers or cyclists resting outside the village inns or admiring the antique shops that occupy the timber-framed buildings of the square. The village becomes very busy in the summer, but even so it does not suffer from the air of commercialism so often found elsewhere.

Church of St Mary, page 63.

In the locality: church at Challock, page 63.

Chillenden

Chillenden Windmill, page 97.

Chislehurst

Chislehurst is a leafy village with large open areas of common and woodland. The powerful Walsingham family lived here in the middle ages and their park, Scadbury, is now a nature reserve and public open space. In the nineteenth century the exiled Louis Napoleon of France, his empress and son came to live in Camden Place (now a golf club). The Imperial eagle may still be seen on buildings in the village, and the Prince Imperial, who was killed in the Zulu Wars, is commemorated by a tall standing cross on the common. The parish church of St Nicholas contains the grave of William Willett (see page 107).

Chislehurst Caves, page 100.

Cobham

Church of St Mary Magdalene, page 63; Cobham Hall, page 70; New College of Cobham, page 75; Owletts, page 76.

Cooling

Cooling Castle, page 53.

Cranbrook

Although the town is not an early one it has an impressive history connected with the growth of the English cloth industry that was centred here in the fourteenth century. This prosperity is reflected throughout the town, which has a wide High Street and substantial church. Until the late nineteenth century the town was frequently cut off by deep mud on the roads each winter and therefore has a rather insular atmosphere. Just off the High Street are the charming museum and the Union Windmill.

Church of St Dunstan, page 63; **Cranbrook Museum**, page 82; **Union Windmill**, page 98.

In the locality: Bedgebury National Pinetum, page 69; Sissinghurst Castle Garden, page 77.

Crayford

David Evans World of Silk, page 100.

Dartford

Early closing Wednesday; market days Thursday and Saturday.

Dartford stands on the Roman Watling Street that linked Kent to London. It is a busy shopping centre with a small collection of old buildings. For centuries it has been an industrial town, with a long history of papermaking. Today it is a popular commuting town. Just outside the town are the Dartford Tunnel under the river Thames and the Queen Elizabeth II Bridge spanning the river. The town museum is well worth a visit, as are the acres of open parkland and heathland, and the Orchard Theatre.

Dartford Borough Museum, page 82.

In the locality: David Evans World of Silk, page 100; Hall Place, page 72; St Johns Jerusalem, page 77.

Deal

Early closing Thursday; market day Saturday.

Deal is a fascinating, mainly eighteenth-century town, full of narrow streets and charming colour-washed houses. It is often referred to as 'Chelsea by the Sea' on account of the many actors and artists who choose to live there. Its association with the sea has been a long one, and Henry VIII built a castle here to defend the coast. The naval dockyard flourished for centuries and in its shelter the town developed as a hot bed of smuggling. The smugglers constructed hides and runs across the rooftops, putting planks over the narrow streets to facilitate quick getaways. The town has several museums and a twentieth-century pier. Each summer street theatres give lively costumed tours of the town, but these must be booked well in advance.

Deal Maritime and Local History Museum, page 82; **Time Ball Tower**, page 83; **Victoriana Exhibition**, page 83.

In the locality: Northbourne Court Garden, page 75; Walmer Castle, page 58; church at Betteshanger, page 60.

Doddington

Church of the Beheading of St John the Baptist, page 63, Doddington Place Gardens, page 71.

Dode

Church of Our Lady of the Meadows, page 64.

Dover

Early closing Wednesday, market days Friday (general), Saturday (fruit and vegetables).

The best way to see Dover is to stand in its castle. From there the steep valley of the river Dour and the extensive harbour are best appreciated. Iron age people would have looked down on a very different scene, with the sea extending right up the valley. The Romans started to embank the estuary and the process has continued up to the present day. As more land was drained houses were erected and the dates of the surviving buildings chart this progress. Dover has been called 'Britain's buried Pompeii' for its wealth of archaeological material. The most impressive site is the Roman Painted House. Tucked away behind Victorian shops is the tiny chapel of St Edmund, founded by St Richard of Chichester in the thirteenth century. It is reputed to be the only surviving religious building dedicated to an English saint that was dedicated by another English saint. It was saved from demolition in the 1960s. On the seafront, overlooking the harbour (built in the twentieth century to house the entire British fleet before the threat of aerial attack made it a bad idea) stands the memorial to Captain Matthew Webb, the first man to swim the Channel. He achieved his ambition in 1875. High on the hill above the town is the memorial to Louis Blériot, who crossed the same stretch of water by air in 1909. In Snargate Street is the famous Grand Shaft Staircase.

Crabble Corn Mill, page 97; **Dover Castle**, page 53; **Dover Museum**, page 83; **Dover Transport Museum**, page 83; **Grand Shaft Staircase**, page 55; **Old Town Gaol**, page 83; **Roman Painted House**, page 54; **White Cliffs Experience**, page 83.

In the locality: Battle of Britain Memorial, page 100; Macfarlane's Butterfly Centre, page 100.

Downe

Darwin Museum, page 85.

At Dover Castle visitors can now see the secret underground tunnels of the Second World War.

Dungeness
Dungeness Power Station, page 101; Old Lighthouse, page 103; RSPB Nature Reserve, page 38.

Dymchurch
The village sits unhappily on the main A259 coast road. It grew up on the sea, but now it is cut off from it by the steady stream of summer traffic. Yet Dymchurch has a character of its own. Many remember it as the setting of Russell Thorndike's Dr Syn mysteries, although a lot has changed since the Thorndikes lived here in the 1920s. The village is a popular holiday resort where some interesting history may be found. The New Hall was built in 1580 as a meeting place for the Lords, Bailiff and Jurats of Romney Marsh. At that time the entire area was centred on Dymchurch. Nearby a martello tower dates from the early nineteenth century. The parish church has a fine Norman doorway and welcomes visitors.

Dymchurch Martello Tower, page 53; **The Law of the Levels**, page 85; **Romney Hythe & Dymchurch Railway**, page 104.

East Malling
East Malling has given its name to many soft fruits, as the Bradbourne Estate in the village, former seat of the Twysden family, is the home of the Centre for Horticultural Research. The centre may best be viewed from the yew-shaded churchyard. There are many footpaths along the valleys carved out by streams, in which watercress grows, past watermills and oast houses and through market gardens. The landscape may not be as dramatic as it is in other parts of Kent, but it is gentle, peaceful countryside that represents all that is best in the Garden of England.

In the locality: Aylesford Priory, page 59; Coldrum Stones, page 49; Great Comp Garden, page 72; St Leonard's Tower, page 52; church at Mereworth, page 65.

Eastwell
Church of St Mary, page 64.

Edenbridge
Although its name suggests a crossing place of the river Eden, the town probably gets its name from a Saxon, Eadhelm, who owned

land here and who built a permanent bridge across the then nameless river. The countryside here is crossed by many streams and dotted with ponds, many of which were dug for the clay used to make the tiles that are be seen on most houses hereabouts. In the centre of the town is Church House, a delightful group of timber-framed buildings now used for community purposes. The church, which stands away from the main road, contains an excellent wooden font cover.

In the locality: Chartwell, page 69; Hever Castle, page 55.

Elham

Parsonage Farm Rural Heritage Centre, page 103; Elham Valley Vineyards, page 105.

Eynsford

One of Kent's picture postcard villages, with its bridge and ford across the river Darent, Eynsford also has a well-preserved castle and a charming church, dating in the main from the thirteenth century.

Eynsford Castle, page 54.

In the locality: Lullingstone Castle, page 73; Lullingstone Park, page 39; Lullingstone Roman Villa, page 49.

Fairfield

Church of St Thomas à Becket, page 64.

Faversham

Early closing day Thursday; market days, Tuesday, Friday and Saturday.

To many people this is the most pleasing small town in Kent, characterised by a wealth of timber-framed houses, many of which are plastered and colour-washed. The Guildhall, built on wooden stilts, still shelters market traders at the junction of the main streets. Arden's House in Abbey Street was the scene of the murder of Thomas Arden in 1551 and is built from the remains of the abbey gatehouse. It was in Faversham Abbey, in 1154, that King Stephen was buried, although nothing remains of the abbey church. Behind Arden's House are the former Elizabethan grammar school and the parish church. The Fleur de Lis Heritage Centre is one of the most interesting in Britain, with a wide range of publications and town trails on sale. A very unusual attraction is a gunpowder mill. Each summer a series of Open House Weekends is organised when two dozen buildings that are not normally open to the public are made accessible. One ticket gives access to all, and a most useful booklet describing the history of the buildings is produced. Telephone the Fleur de Lis Heritage Centre (01795 534542) for further information.

Chart Gunpowder Mill, page 97; **church of St Mary of Charity**, page 65; **Fleur de Lis Heritage Centre**, page 85.

In the locality: Brogdale Orchards, page 100; Farming World, page 101; Mount Ephraim Gardens, page 75.

Folkestone

Early closing days Wednesday and Saturday; market day Sunday.

During the nineteenth century Folkestone was Kent's most fashionable resort, owing its success to the coming of the railway and the patronage of the Earl of Radnor. The Leas, a broad swathe of grass on top of the cliff, is overlooked by genteel hotels, whilst what remains of the fishing town sprawls down the hill to the harbour. The parish church stands on the hill and contains the shrine of St Eanswith, a local princess and granddaughter of King Ethelbert, who founded a monastery here in the seventh century. A later resident of the town was William Harvey, the seventeenth-century physician who discovered the circulation of the blood. A statue on the clifftop commemorates him. There is a very good local history museum whilst the Martello Tower Centre is outside the town. Visitors are able to use the second oldest cliff lift in Britain, opened in 1885, to climb the tall cliffs overlooking the beach. It still uses its original water balance system.

Folkestone Museum, page 85; **Martello Tower Visitors' Centre,** page 102.

In the locality: Battle of Britain Memorial, page 100; Kent Battle of Britain Museum, page 86.

Fordwich

This charming little village is situated so close

The bandstand at Folkestone.

to Canterbury that it has been ignored for far too long. Until the river Stour silted up it was one of the main ports for Canterbury, but it is difficult today to picture it bustling with commerce. Red brick and flint walls jostle with timber-framed buildings grouped around the medieval church and town hall.

Fordwich Town Hall, page 85.

Gillingham

Market days Monday and Saturday.

The town owes its existence to the nearby river Medway and was home to most of the workers in the nearby Chatham Dockyard until its closure. With industrial growth the town now has a new business park and sprawling housing estates that are gradually filling the gap between the river and the motorway. The river has recently been the subject of much regeneration, with a country park, riverside gardens and open-air pool provided. There are good walks from which shipping may be observed. In the sixteenth century Will Adams was born in the town. He trav-

elled to Japan and became the first English-man to set foot there. As advisor to the rulers of Japan he became a prominent citizen and built English-style ships for the Japanese. A clock-tower was erected to his memory in the 1930s and may be found on the A2 not far from the site of Jezreel's Tower (see page 108).

Royal Engineers Museum, page 86.

Godmersham

A tiny village set in some of the best country-side between Canterbury and Ashford, Godmersham is famous because Jane Austen's brother Edward lived here in the magnificent surroundings of Godmersham Park. The mansion house is now the headquarters of a major company which maintains the grounds superbly and occasionally opens them in aid of charity. The parish church was much restored in the nineteenth century by the eminent architect William Butterfield and has work of the pre-Conquest period on display.

Goodnestone

Goodnestone Park Gardens, page 71.

Goudhurst

Early closing Wednesday.

William Cobbett wrote in 1823: 'I came to Goudhurst, which stands upon one of the steepest hills in this part of the country.' Indeed it does, and the High Street tumbles down from the parish church to the duckpond at the bottom. The houses in the main street are of great interest. The large house opposite the Star and Eagle Inn saw the birth of the Rootes Motor Group, when William Rootes opened a cycle repair shop there in about 1900. It had been a barracks during the Napoleonic Wars. At the top of the hill, overlooking the churchyard, is a fine row of weavers' cottages. An exceptionally well-preserved hall house, Pattyndenne Manor, is open to groups

The statue of Pocahontas in St George's churchyard at Gravesend.

by appointment (telephone: 01580 211361). The church of St Mary is a fine medieval building.

Bedgebury National Pinetum, page 69; **church of St Mary**, page 65; **Finchcocks**, page 71.

In the locality: Cranbrook Museum, page 82; Owl House Gardens, page 76; Scotney Castle, page 57; church at Kilndown, page 65.

Gravesend

Early closing Wednesday; market day Saturday, indoor market daily.

The name derives from 'Grove's End' so is not as sinister as it sounds. Gravesend is the place where pilots board vessels on their inbound journeys to London, and life still depends on the river. There is a foot passenger ferry to Tilbury in Essex. Gravesend suffered a serious fire in the eighteenth century so there are few old buildings. On the promenade is the fort, originally built for Henry VIII, but much altered in the nineteenth century. Nearby is the medieval Milton Chantry. General Charles Gordon of Khartoum lived in the town for six years whilst he was in charge of New Tavern Fort and he was a generous benefactor, especially amongst the poor boys of the town. There is a splendid statue of him in Fort Gardens, cast by Doulton. The narrow High Street contains the town hall, behind which is a flourishing market. At nearby St George's church the Red Indian princess Pocahontas was buried in 1617, although the present church is not the building that was there at the time. She was the first American Indian to visit Britain, but died on her journey home, whilst her ship was moored at Gravesend.

Chantry Heritage Centre, page 86; **New Tavern Fort**, page 56.

In the locality: Cobham Hall, page 70; Gad's Hill, page 71; Milton Chantry, page 66; New College of Cobham, page 75; Owletts, page 76.

Greatstone

Dunrobin Stud Farm, page 101.

Groombridge

Groombridge Place Gardens, page 72.

Hadlow

Hadlow is a busy little village on the main road between Tonbridge and Maidstone. Travellers cannot fail to see its most famous building, Hadlow Tower, built in the nineteenth century as the crowning glory of Hadlow Court Castle. Whilst the castle itself has been demolished, the tower survives and has been converted into a single house. From the churchyard you get a good view that shows that it is built of brick covered with stucco – a common deceit in the nineteenth century when dressed stone was the most popular building material and brick the most common! The church of St Mary is dwarfed by the tower and stands at the end of a pretty little cul-de-sac. The nineteenth-century brewery has been converted into apartments and has brought much life back to the village centre, which has been further enhanced by the installation of a brick road instead of tarmac. Just outside the village is the renowned Hadlow Agricultural College, whose garden centre is well worth a visit.

In the locality: Old Soar Manor, page 76; Tonbridge Castle, page 57; Whitbread Hop Farm, page 79; Yalding Organic Gardens, page 78.

Harty

One of the most isolated villages in Kent, Harty is the place to go for solitude and a deep sense of history. Reached down a single-track road across marshes from the road between Eastchurch and Leysdown on the Isle of Sheppey, Harty was once a more prosperous place when a ferry boat ran across the river Swale. Now the ferry runs no more and only fishermen, birdwatchers and walkers find their way here. The tiny church, dedicated to St Thomas of Canterbury, houses a rare Flemish chest carved with scenes of a joust; it is usually open to the public. Nearby, with views across the Swale, is the Ferry Inn, where in the winter one could easily imagine Miss Marple arriving to solve a mysterious crime. There are few places in the county so full of atmosphere.

In the locality: Minster Gatehouse Museum, page 91.

Hawkinge

Kent Battle of Britain Museum, page 86.

Headcorn

Headcorn is a popular village with many picturesque houses and shops. The dog-leg High Street has been the subject of recent enhancement schemes and is always busy. At one corner is the large parish church, which benefited from the cloth industry here in the late medieval period. In its churchyard are the remains of one of the oldest oak trees in Britain. Headcorn is now a popular commuter settlement, with easy rail links to London and to the continent via Ashford International.

Headcorn Flower Centre and Vineyard, pages 102 and 105; **Lashenden Air Warfare Museum**, page 87.

In the locality: Iden Croft Herbs, page 102; Sissinghurst Castle Garden, page 77.

Herne Bay

Early closing Thursday; market day Saturday.

This pleasant town was established in the nineteenth century as a planned resort with squares and gardens. Its promenade can be very windy in winter, but the town is full of atmosphere. The Pier was severely damaged by storms in the 1950s. A major concert venue, the King's Hall, stands at the east end of the promenade where grassy slopes run down to the sea, whilst sheltered formal sunken gardens have been restored. The clock-tower is unusual in that it was the tallest purpose-built clock-tower in the world when it was built in 1837. Today it still dominates the front. In the 1990s a series of contemporary sculptures, unsurpassed in south-east England, was erected in the High Street and along the Sea Front on the initiative of the local council.

Brambles English Wildlife and Rare Breeds, page 100; **Herne Bay Museum**, page 87; **Herne Windmill**, page 98.

In the locality: Reculver Roman Fort, page 50.

Hever

Hever Castle, page 55.

Higham
Gad's Hill, page 71.

Hollingbourne
Church of All Saints, page 65.

Hythe
Early closing Wednesday.
Hythe is one of the Cinque Ports and still retains its old world atmosphere along the narrow High Street and in the lanes near the church. Beneath the east end of the church is a crypt containing hundreds of human skulls and other bones, removed from the church-yard during clearances to allow for new buri-als. The crypt is open to the public at set times during the summer. In the north-west corner of the churchyard is the grave of Lionel Lukin, who invented the lifeboat. The Royal Military Canal runs through the town and is the setting for a biannual Venetian Festival. The sea which gave Hythe its medieval prosperity has receded but has left the town full of char-acter. The Romney Hythe & Dymchurch Light Railway has its terminus to the west of the town centre.

Hythe Local History Room, page 87; **Hythe Watermill**, page 98; **Romney Hythe & Dymchurch Railway**, page 104.

In the locality: Lympne Castle, page 56; Port Lympne Wild Animal Park, page 104.

The High Street, Hythe.

Ickham
Church of St John the Evangelist, page 65.

Ide Hill
Emmetts Garden, page 71.

Ightham
Ightham Mote, page 72; Oldbury Hillfort, page 50.

Kilndown
Christ Church, page 65.

Lamberhurst
Lamberhurst Vineyard, page 105; Owl House Gardens, page 76; Scotney Castle, page 57.

Leeds
Leeds Castle, page 56.

Leigh
Leigh is very much an estate village with many brick and timber-framed houses of the nineteenth century, built by the Morley fam-ily of Hall Place. The large gates stand on a little green next to the parish church and speak of Victorian wealth. The whole village is pic-turesque and the church contains one of the few remaining Elizabethan hourglass stands, used to time sixteenth-century sermons.

In the locality: Chiddingstone Castle, page 70; Hever Castle, page 55; Penshurst Place, page 76.

Lenham
Village squares are not a feature of Kent, which is better known for its greens and open spaces. Lenham has a charming market square surrounded by timber-framed houses and eighteenth-century brickwork, with some noted inns and restaurants. On one side of the square is the large parish church, which dis-

The George Inn and High Street at Lydd.

plays a good Elizabethan pulpit, some enormous wooden doors into the tower and some good monuments. The village also has an eighteenth-century lockup and some good examples of medieval farm buildings.

In the locality: Leeds Castle, page 56.

Leysdown-on-Sea

A popular resort with far more of interest than its 1950s image appears to offer, Leysdown grew as a result of a light railway which ran from Sheerness across the Isle of Sheppey. It consists mainly of caravan, chalet and mobile home parks. Large family groups, particularly from the East End of London, found it an enchanting place and several generations later their descendants still come for their traditional holidays. Apart from the inevitable amusement parks there are some of the cleanest beaches in southeast England, a coastal country park and an official naturist beach 2 miles (3 km) south of the village at the charming hamlet of Shellness.

In the locality: Minster Abbey Gatehouse Museum, page 91.

Loose

Although now a suburb of Maidstone, Loose still retains its own identity, being set in a narrow valley with quiet walks on causeways along the sides of crystal-clear streams. The tranquil appearance is misleading, however, as this was one of the most heavily industrialised areas of Kent, with several dozen watermills along a short stretch of river. Many were corn and fulling mills but the majority were built for papermaking, taking advantage of the purity of the water. The church is predominantly nineteenth-century but looks extremely pretty situated above the stream, whilst the viaduct which carries the main road from Maidstone is one of the few buildings in Kent by Thomas Telford, constructed in 1829. The Old Wool House in Wells Street, a timber-framed building of fifteenth-century date, is now owned by the National Trust and is open to the public by written appointment during the summer.

In the locality: Boughton Monchelsea

Place, page 69; Stoneacre, page 78.

Lullingstone

Lullingstone Castle, page 73; Lullingstone Roman Villa, page 49.

Lydd

In the nineteenth century a new explosive was tested in this area and named 'lyddite'. Fifty years later an airport was constructed just outside the town and today the landscape is marred by pylons running from the nearby Dungeness Power Station. For all that, Lydd is a very pleasant place, with an enormous parish church whose west tower was started by Thomas Wolsey, later to become famous as a cardinal. In 1940 a bomb destroyed the chancel and the opportunity was taken to re-build it in thirteenth-century style more in keeping with the rest of the building. It was a great success and is worth a special journey to see. There is a large collection of memorial brasses and the remains of the pre-Conquest church are to be seen at the west end.

Lydd Town Museum, page 87.

In the locality: Dungeness Power Station, page 103; Old Dungeness Lighthouse, page 101; Philippine Village Craft Centre, page 104; church at Fairfield, page 64.

Lympne

Lympne Castle, page 56; Port Lympne Wild Animal Park, page 104.

Maidstone

Early closing Wednesday; market day Tuesday.

Maidstone is the county town of Kent and a market has been held there each Tuesday since 1261. Today it is an important regional shopping centre, and all the buildings in the town centre reflect this, rather than their history. However, tucked away are some interesting buildings. Next to All Saints' church are the former stables that now house a carriage museum. The Archbishop's Palace opposite now houses the register office. William Hazlitt, the essayist, was born in Earl Street in 1778. His father was Unitarian minister at the church that still stands in Market Buildings. In Week Street is a good example of pargeting – painted and moulded plasterwork decorating the front wall of a building.

Within the Borough of Maidstone are several villages. Penenden Heath is still the picturesque open space on which public meetings and executions were held until the nineteenth century. The first recorded lawsuit in English history took place there in 1076. On the other side of the town is Mote Park, a large public open space with many sporting facilities and a large lake. In the town centre are the Museum and Art Gallery and the County Archives Office. The Museum of Kent Life, 2 miles (3 km) from the town centre, may be easily reached by car or bus.

Maidstone Museum and Art Gallery, page 90; **Museum of Kent Life**, page 90; **Tyland Barn**, page 105; **Tyrwhitt-Drake Museum of Carriages**, page 90.

In the locality: Boughton Monchelsea Place, page 69.

Manston

RAF Manston Hurricane and Spitfire Memorial Building, page 90.

Margate

Early closing Thursday; market day Monday.

Margate is one of the oldest resorts in Kent. During the eighteenth century the first bathing machines in the county were used here and fashionable guesthouses sprang up. The town was convenient for visitors coming by boat from London, and later the railway made it easier still. The nineteenth-century pier has been destroyed, but there is much to do. Dreamland Theme Park has been doing good business for over sixty years. Tucked away from the seafront are the interesting Old Town Hall Museum, the Shell Grotto and Margate Caves, whilst Draper's Mill stands a little outside the centre. A remarkable medieval house, Salmestone Grange, stands on the edge of the town near the cemetery and is open to the public by prior appointment; its chapel is used each Sunday.

Draper's Windmill, page 98; **Dreamland Theme Park**, page 101; **Margate Caves**, page 102; **Old Town Hall Museum**, page 91; **Shell Grotto**, page 104.

Overlooking Margate Bay is the memorial to the crew of the surf boat 'Friends of All Nations', lost in 1897.

In the locality: Bleak House Museum, page 79; Dickens House Museum, page 80; Minster Abbey, page 66; Quex House, page 76.

Matfield

This is a charming village, the epitome of the country scene. The large house, green and duck pond form a picturesque group whilst the nearby teashop provides a warm welcome. Siegfried Sassoon lived in the village and his gaunt house on the road to Paddock Wood is marked by a plaque. The gardens of Crittenden House nearby are occasionally open to the public.

Badsell Park Farm, page 100.

Meopham

Meopham Windmill, page 98.

Mereworth

Church of St Lawrence, page 65.

Milton Regis

Court Hall Museum, page 91.

Minster in Sheppey

Minster Abbey, page 66; Minster Abbey Gatehouse Museum, page 91.

Minster in Thanet

Minster Abbey , page 66.

Newenden

Church of St Peter, page 66.

New Romney

Early closing Wednesday; market day Friday.

The sea used to lap against the southern wall of the churchyard (the old shoreline is easily detected by a change in ground level) but in 1287 a severe storm threw up shingle and forced the river Rother, which originally entered the sea here, to divert several miles to the west. The town was swamped by a tidal wave and the church flooded to a depth of many feet. Even today the pillars are stained, and the building now stands in a hollow, giving some indication of how much shingle was thrown up by the storm. The town has some interesting examples of medieval architecture, and it was formerly one of the wealthiest ports in the land. Just outside the town is the Romney Hythe & Dymchurch Railway.

Romney Hythe & Dymchurch Railway, page 104.

In the locality: Dunrobin Stud Farm, page 101; The Law of the Levels, page 85; Lydd Town Museum, page 87; church at Brookland, page 61.

Nurstead

A church and manor house are all that stand at Nurstead between Gravesend and Meopham. The church dates in the main from the thirteenth century and is a good example of a church of a small agricultural community. It contains monuments to the Edmeades family, who have lived in Nurstead Court for over four hundred years. The house itself is a fragment of an unusual aisled hall-house of fourteenth-century date, built for a Bishop of London. Bed and breakfast accommodation is offered in this wonderful family home, which is also open to small groups by appointment (telephone: 01474 812121).

In the locality: Chantry Heritage Centre, page 86; Cobham Hall, page 70; Meopham Windmill, page 98; Owletts, page 76; and church at Cobham, page 63.

Orpington
Early closing Thursday.

The remains of Orpington Priory stand in some charming gardens just off the busy High Street. Although there is little to see they are a reminder that this is an ancient town and a Roman villa has been excavated by the railway station. With excellent rail links to London it has become prime commuter territory, sacrificing some of its character in the process. However, it is on the very edge of suburbia and is a good centre from which to explore the open countryside nearby. The Walnuts Sports and Shopping Centre is a well-planned development in the town centre that is encouraging people to stay in Orpington for their leisure even if they leave it to go to work.

Bromley Museum, page 91; **Crofton Roman Villa**, page 49.

Ospringe
Maison Dieu, page 74.

Otford

The chief feature of interest in Otford is the ruined palace that stands in water-meadows to the south of the church. Built by Archbishop Warham in about 1510, it later passed, with many church properties, to King Henry

The Archbishop's Palace at Otford is where Henry VIII stayed on his way to the Field of the Cloth of Gold near Calais.

VIII, and within a few years was a ruin. To-day only a small part remains, but the impressive brick tower reminds us that Henry stayed here with a retinue of four thousand on his way to the Field of the Cloth of Gold. The village clusters around the village pond, whilst the church is tucked away in a corner. It contains one of the largest collections of funeral hatchments in the county. These were coats of arms carried at the funerals of members of arms-bearing families in the seventeenth and eighteenth centuries. There are many good walks to be taken from Otford, either along the Pilgrims' Way or in the Darent valley.

In the locality: Eynsford Castle, page 54; Knole, page 73; Lullingstone Castle, page 73; Lullingstone Roman Villa, page 49.

Otham

Stoneacre, page 78.

Patrixbourne

Church of St Mary, page 66.

Penshurst

This sleepy little village is overshadowed by its famous mansion and church, both of which are hidden away from the road. The approach to the church is picturesque through a nineteenth-century archway at the end of Leicester Square. Fine walks are to be had using the village as a base and excellent views may be obtained by walking towards Bidborough.

Penshurst Place, page 76; **Penshurst Vineyard**, page 105.

In the locality: Chiddingstone Castle, page 70; Hever Castle, page 55.

Plaxtol

Old Soar Manor, page 76.

Pluckley

Until it became the setting for the popular television series *The Darling Buds of May* Pluckley was famous only for its pretty parish church, often referred to as the most haunted in England. Indeed, ghosts are said to be found all over the village, apparently finding something here that they do not get elsewhere. Many of the houses in the village have round-headed windows – a local characteristic. Tradition says that it was through a window of this shape that the lord of the manor escaped during the English Civil War and that he later had similar ones installed in all estate properties as a thanksgiving. The village now receives numerous tourists eager to seek out the locations used for the television series, but they are privately owned and not open to the public. However, quietness prevails for most of the year and a visit is recommended, especially in the spring when thousands of daffodils welcome the traveller.

In the locality: Godinton House, page 71.

Queenborough

This is a little town of much character. Whilst it could not be described as 'pretty' it has a great history and a worthwhile half-hour can be spent exploring its streets. The town was founded in the reign of Edward III and named in honour of his wife. The unusual castle is now no more than a bank and ditch system near the railway station, although the visitor to the fascinating parish church will see a carved representation of it on the font, with its cannon blazing! The churchyard merits exploration, for the town served to house officers from the former royal dockyard at Sheerness, and the gravestones record the world travels of many lives. The pretty Guildhall dates from the eighteenth century, whilst the little creek behind the main street is still busy with small craft.

In the locality: Minster Abbey Gatehouse Museum, page 91.

Ramsgate

Early closing Thursday; market day Friday.
The harbour bustles with yachts, the main streets have busy shops and the tall cliffs have bracing walks. The town prides itself on its aristocratic past; visitors have included George IV, Jane Austen, Elizabeth Fry, Baroness Burdett-Coutts and Vincent Van Gogh. Augustus Welby Pugin (1812-52), the nineteenth-century architect, built himself a house here on the West Cliff. It is private but next to it is the Abbey Church of St Augustine which he built and in which he is buried. Here his architecture and stained glass may be appreci-

ated as in no other church in southern England. In the grounds of East Cliff Lodge is a remarkable Italianate greenhouse built in 1805.

Ramsgate Model Village, page 104; **Ramsgate Museum**, page 91.

In the locality: Bleak House Museum, page 79; Dickens House Museum, page 80; RAF Manston Hurricane and Spitfire Memorial Building, page 90; Richborough Castle, page 51;

Reculver

Roman Fort and Saxon Church, page 50.

Richborough

Richborough Castle, page 51.

Rochester

Early closing Wednesday; market day Friday; flea market Saturday.

Dominated by its castle and cathedral, Rochester is a bustling city best explored on foot. An interesting walking tour may start at the castle, the keep of which dates from 1127. Fine views may be obtained from the battlements. On the Esplanade is the **Bridge Chapel**, erected in 1397 for medieval travellers to give thanks for the stone bridge. There are now two road bridges across the Medway, dating from 1914 and 1971, still maintained by the Bridge Trust. Just round the corner in the High Street is the **Bull Hotel**, featured by Charles Dickens in two of his novels (see page 106). Opposite is the **Guildhall** built in the seventeenth century. The main council chamber, with an elaborate plaster ceiling, is now open to the public as part of the excellent museum. A little further along the High Street

Plan of Rochester, showing the route of the walk suggested in the text. 1 Castle. 2 Bridge Chapel. 3 Bull Hotel. 4 Guildhall. 5 Corn Exchange. 6 Chertseys Gate. 7 Blackboys Alley. 8 Six Poor Travellers' House. 9 City walls. 10 Charles Dickens Centre. 11 Restoration House. 12 The Vines. 13 Minor Canon Row. 14 Cathedral.

ROCHESTER

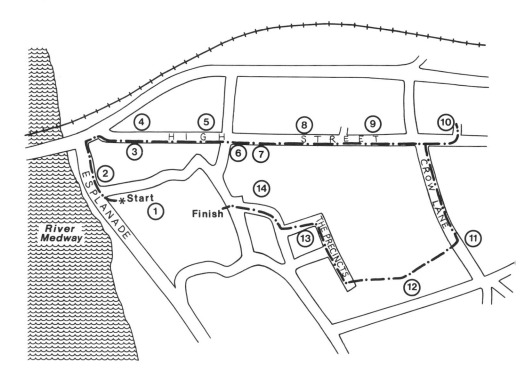

is the **Corn Exchange**, dominated by a gilded clock. The building was the gift of Sir Cloudesley Shovell in 1706. **Chertseys Gate** is a fine fifteenth-century gateway to the cathedral precinct, built of banded flint and stone, although the timber-framed house above is of a later date. A few yards further on is **Blackboys Alley**, leading to the north door of the cathedral. Pilgrims used this route to visit the shrine of St William of Perth. On the opposite side of the street is the **Six Poor Travellers' House**. At the large car park the **city wall** is reached, with the foundation of the former gateway picked out in different stones across the road. **Eastgate House** is now the Charles Dickens Centre whilst the charming gardens behind contain the chalet in which Dickens did much of his writing. It was brought here after his death. In Crow Lane **Restoration House** is a sixteenth-century brick mansion where Charles II stayed on his restoration to the monarchy in 1660. It overlooks **The Vines**, a stately park laid out on the site of the medieval monks' vineyard. At the western end are two eighteenth-century houses with excellent examples of fire insurance marks on their walls. The Precincts then leads into **Minor Canon Row**, built in the eighteenth century for cathedral staff. The actress Dame Sybil Thorndike lived here in the early part of the twentieth century.

The city has two extremely popular Dickens festivals, one in early summer, the other in December, when it is common for the streets to be filled with people in period costume. A wide range of events is planned and programmes are available from the tourist information centre.

Charles Dickens Centre, page 91; **Guildhall Museum,** page 91; **Rochester Castle**, page 56; **Rochester Cathedral**, page 67; **Poor Travellers' House**, page 92.

In the locality: Chatham Historic Dockyard, page 82; Gad's Hill, page 71; Temple Manor, page 78; Theatre Royal, page 105; Upnor Castle, page 58.

Rolvenden
Booth Historic Vehicle Collection, page 92; Great Maytham Hall, page 72.

The seventeenth-century Guildhall in Rochester.

St Margaret's Bay
The Bay Museum, page 92; The Pines Gardens, page 76; South Foreland Lighthouse, page 105.

St Nicholas at Wade
Church of St Nicholas, page 67.

Sandgate
Sandgate Castle, page 57.

Sandwich
Early closing Wednesday; market day Thursday.

Sandwich is not typical of Kent. Its medieval walls survive in part and the layout of its streets has hardly changed in centuries. The town has more listed buildings per head of population than any other in England – with a total of 435. At its heart is the Guildhall, originally built in 1579. Three medieval churches are of great interest and all are open to the public. The Salutation, a mansion built by Sir Edwin Lutyens in 1911, may be glimpsed from the footpath. Its gardens were laid out to make the most of the townscape. One of the most picturesque corners of the town is the Quay, with its Barbican Gateway. A toll road leads to Sandwich Bay, a private estate of large houses with marvellous sandy beaches, the Royal St George's Golf Club and nature reserves. The town has two museums and a windmill.

Church of St Peter, page 67; **Precinct Toy Collection**, page 92; **Sandwich Museum**, page 94; **White Mill**, page 99.

In the locality: Goodnestone Park Gardens, page 71; Minster Abbey, page 66; Richborough Castle, page 51; church at Betteshanger, page 60.

Sarre
Sarre Windmill, page 98.

Scotney
Scotney Castle, page 57.

Sevenoaks
Early closing Wednesday; market days Wednesday and Saturday.
The town stands on a sandstone ridge that forms a ripple along the edge of the Weald of Kent. The old part of the town, comprising the church, manor house, school and almshouses, stands slightly apart from the more recent commercial area and suffers from traffic despite an early bypass. Next to the church is The Chantry, a fine seventeenth-century brick house. Not far away is The Red House, formerly the home of Jane Austen's great uncle, whom she frequently visited. To the east of the main street lies the great expanse of Knole Park, which is open throughout the year. The house is open in the summer. The Vine, at the north end of the town, is a cricket field where the game has been played for at least two hundred years.

Knole, page 73; **Riverhill House Gardens**, page 77; **Sevenoaks Museum**, page 94; **Sevenoaks Wildfowl Reserve**, page 43.

In the locality: Emmetts Garden, page 71; Ightham Mote, page 72.

Sheerness
Market days Tuesday and Saturday.
The town grew up around a naval dockyard laid out by Samuel Pepys in the 1660s but closed three hundred years later. Today it is a major port and ferry terminal. The town makes a good centre from which to explore the Isle of Sheppey. In the centre of the island is Minster, which has an interesting abbey and museum. On the road between Sheerness and Minster is the famous Ship on Shore, a folly constructed in the nineteenth century from solidified concrete barrels salvaged from a wreck.

In the locality: Minster Abbey, page 66; Minster Abbey Gatehouse Museum, page 91.

Shoreham
A pretty little village on the river Darent, Shoreham is dominated by a chalk cross cut high in the hillside. The countryside here is familiar through the paintings of Samuel Palmer, who lived in this valley for six years, and the writings of his friend William Blake. Still largely undiscovered by tourists, the village is a sleeping beauty with plenty to offer those who seek the unspoilt rural England so well portrayed by its former residents.

The Hop Shop, page 102.

In the locality: Darwin Museum, page 85; Eynsford Castle, page 54; Lullingstone Castle, page 73; Lullingstone Roman Villa, page 49.

Sissinghurst
Sissinghurst Castle Garden, page 77.

Sittingbourne
Early closing Wednesday; market days Friday and Saturday.
Much has changed since Henry V stayed in the area on his way to Agincourt. Industrialisation has taken over and as a result there are few interesting old buildings left. The bustling High Street has a wide variety of shops and the parish church, which dates mainly from the thirteenth century, provides a quiet oasis, although restorations of the eighteenth

and nineteenth centuries were not kind to it. The nearby village of Milton Regis has kept a larger proportion of its old buildings including the medieval Court Hall. The Sittingbourne & Kemsley Light Railway is nearby.

Court Hall Museum, page 91; **Sittingbourne & Kemsley Light Railway**, page 104.

Smallhythe

Smallhythe Place, page 77.

Smarden

This is an ideal village in which to study medieval architecture. The fourteenth-century church is tucked away behind some of the most attractive timber-framed houses in the Weald. Smarden prospered in the middle ages after being granted a market charter by Edward III in 1332.

Speldhurst

Church of St Mary the Virgin, page 68.

Staplehurst

Brattle Farm Museum, page 94; Iden Croft Herbs, page 102.

Stelling Minnis

Stelling Minnis Windmill, page 99.

Strood

Temple Manor, page 78.

Tenterden

Early closing Wednesday; market day Friday.

The wide High Street is a reminder that cattle markets used to be held there. The town is little changed, having escaped the nineteenth-century practice of building new houses near the railway. This was because the railway was late in arriving. The station is now the headquarters of the Kent & East Sussex Railway. The fine town hall with its impressive façade contains a memorable council chamber which may often be viewed on application to the tourist information centre. There is an excellent museum. Many of the houses in the town are weatherboarded or clad in mathematical tiles, a neat way of covering timber-

framed houses in the nineteenth century.

Kent & East Sussex Railway, page 102; **Tenterden Vineyards**, page 105.

In the locality: Great Maytham Hall, page 72; Smallhythe Place, page 77.

Tonbridge

Early closing Wednesday; market day Saturday, flea market Friday.

A town grew here near the crossing of the river Medway in the years before the Norman Conquest. In its centre stands the castle, built to defend the whole area. Whilst Tonbridge is not a pretty town, it has superb open spaces close to the High Street, bounded by tributaries of the Medway. Boats may be hired and many other sports are catered for, both indoors and outdoors. There are many good public houses. The well-known school was founded in 1553.

Tonbridge Castle, page 57.

In the locality: Ightham Mote, page 72; Penshurst Place, page 76; Riverhill House Gardens, page 77; Yalding Organic Gardens, page 78.

Trottiscliffe

Church of St Peter and St Paul, page 68; Coldrum Stones, page 49.

Tunbridge Wells

Early closing Wednesday; market day Wednesday.

The wells were discovered by Lord North in 1606. A sickly man, he lived to the age of eighty-five, no doubt sustained by the many glasses of mineral water he drank! Today the waters may be still be drunk from the town's official dipper during the summer. After the visit of Queen Henrietta Maria guesthouses were built and a town became established, taking its name from the nearest existing town of Tonbridge (the spelling was later changed to avoid confusion). In 1684 a chapel, dedicated to King Charles the Martyr, was built for the use of those who stayed in the area for the season. By the end of the seventeenth century the town was a very popular resort. From 1735 the famous Beau Nash was Master of Ceremonies at the wells, and whilst Tunbridge Wells did not achieve the same

The Pantiles at Tunbridge Wells now house the visitor attraction 'A Day at the Wells'.

level of popularity as some other spas it did become an important regional centre. Today the spa overlooks The Pantiles, an arcade of shops first built in the seventeenth century. The exhibition 'A Day at the Wells' may be found here, whilst the museum, theatre and modern shopping centre are located on top of the hill. Acres of common land close to the town centre provide excellent walks, and High Rocks, a popular Victorian pleasure ground with an inn, have been restored and are well worth a visit.

Tunbridge Wells Museum and Art Gallery, page 94; **A Day at the Wells**, page 94.

In the locality: Penshurst Place, page 76; Tonbridge Castle, page 57; church at Speldhurst, page 68.

Upnor
Upnor Castle, page 58.

Waldershare
Church of All Saints, page 68.

Walmer
Walmer Castle, page 58.

Westerham
Early closing Wednesday.
Few villages have such an impressive list of past residents. Pitt, Wolfe and Churchill have all been associated with Westerham. Yet the village would be of interest even without their fame. Its green is a sloping site of great charm with the parish church tucked away in a corner. It contains an extremely early royal arms of King Edward VI, dating from the sixteenth century. At one end of the village is the delightful Squerryes Court, whilst at the other end is Quebec House, home of General Wolfe. Chartwell, the home of Sir Winston Churchill, stands some miles from the village.

Chartwell, page 69; **Quebec House**, page 76; **Squerryes Court**, page 78.

In the locality: Emmetts Garden, page 71.

West Malling
Early closing Wednesday and Thursday.
West Malling is the only village in Kent to have three Norman towers. One is on the parish church, another forms part of the Abbey, whilst the third is a defensive structure in the nearby hamlet of St Leonard's. The Abbey is occupied

Town houses around the churchyard in the centre of Ashford.

Pretty weatherboarded cottages in Eynsford.

by Anglican nuns and is not open to the public, although most of the buildings may be seen from the delightful Swan Street. The High Street is extremely wide, showing that a market was formerly held here. Adjoining the end of the High Street is Manor Farm Country Park.

Manor Farm Country Park, page 39; **St Leonard's Tower**, page 52.

In the locality: Coldrum Stones, page 49; Great Comp Garden, page 72; Nepicar Farm, page 102; church at Mereworth, page 65.

West Peckham
Church of St Dunstan, page 68.

Whitstable
Early closing Wednesday; market day Thursday.

The town has great charm and grew up around its small harbour, famous for its oyster fishery. A well-established Oyster Festival is held each summer. There are few old buildings but the small church at Seasalter is the remnant of a medieval building of much larger size. There are pleasant walks along miles of deserted beach, much loved by the actor Peter Cushing, who made this town his home. A unique walk is along the former 'Crab and Winkle Line' (see page 38). On the Island Wall is the *Favourite*, built as an oyster yawl in 1890 and restored since 1977 by a charitable trust. Visitors should not miss one of the most unusual cinemas in Britain, housed in the Royal Native Oyster Stores at Horsebridge. Equipped with the latest sound system and boasting the most leg-room in Kent, it has greatly enhanced

the town's reputation as an all-weather resort.

Whitstable Museum and Gallery, page 95; **Whitstable Oyster and Fishery Museum**, page 95.

Wingham
Church of St Mary, page 68; Wingham Bird Park, page 105.

Wittersham
Stocks Mill, page 99.

Woodchurch
Woodchurch Windmill, page 99.

Wrotham
Nepicar Farm, page 102.

Wye
Wye is a charming village which since 1892 has housed the Agricultural College of the University of London. Many of the college buildings are medieval and formed part of the educational establishment founded by Cardinal Kempe, who lived nearby. There are some well-preserved houses of the sixteenth and seventeenth centuries in the streets that radiate from the parish church. Much of the church was lost in 1686 when its central tower collapsed, but it has a special charm. Overlooking the village, on the Downs, is a chalk crown cut in 1902 to commemorate the coronation of Edward VII. Fine views may be obtained from the nature reserve.

Wye National Nature Reserve, page 47.
In the locality: church at Eastwell, page 64.

By the oyster yawl 'Favourite' in Whitstable is a 'grotter' of shells for public donations.

3
The countryside

Whilst Kent benefits from twelve long-distance footpaths, it is in the smaller and less disturbed areas of countryside that its beauty and natural history may best be discovered. Both the Kent Wildlife Trust (Tyland Barn, Chatham Road, Sandling, Maidstone; telephone 01622 662012; see also page 105) and the County Council (Access and Recreation Officer, Planning Department, Kent County Council, Maidstone ME14 2LX) actively encourage the use of the countryside and provide excellent facilities.

Bedgebury National Pinetum, Goudhurst (OS 188: TQ 715338). See page 69.

Bewl Water, Lamberhurst, Tunbridge Wells TN3 8JH (OS 188: TQ 678339). Telephone: 01892 890661. Off A21 1 mile (1.6 km) south of Lamberhurst.

Bewl Water lies in the High Weald Area of Outstanding Natural Beauty. 17 miles (27 km) of picturesque woodland and meadow encircle the lake, which covers 770 acres (310 hectares) and is the largest area of inland water in the south-east of England. There is a wide variety of attractions including a passenger ferry boat that operates during the summer and a visitor centre with an eighty-seat restaurant and an exciting woodland playground for children. Other activities on offer include trout fishing, club sailing and windsurfing.

Bluebell Hill Picnic Site, Chatham (OS 178 and 188: TQ 744622). A quarter of a mile (400 metres) west of A229, 3 miles (5 km) south of Chatham.

The finest views across the Medway valley may be obtained from this point where a car park has been formed on the edge of the escarpment. The valley below has been scarred by industry but this open area of downland has changed little. The open space forms part of the route of the North Downs Way.

Bough Beech Nature Reserve, Ide Hill (OS 188: TQ 495494). 2 miles (3 km) south of Ide Hill. Telephone for further information: 01622 662012.

The formation of Bough Beech reservoir was completed in 1969. It is filled from the river Eden during the winter and gradually empties during the summer. Many species of waterfowl may be found here and there is an interesting visitor centre with displays on the history and natural history of the area. A public footpath runs into the surrounding countryside, whilst the best views of the reservoir may be obtained from the northern end of the causeway.

Brockhill Country Park, Sandling Road, Saltwood, Hythe CT21 4HL (OS 179 and 189: TR 145360). Telephone: 01303 266327.

This picturesque country park with views towards the sea opened in 1986. It covers 54 acres (22 hectares) and there is a waymarked circular walk. Attractions include a lake, a waterfall and stream, barbecue and play areas, information centre and refreshment kiosk.

Brookland Lakes, Snodland (OS 178 and 188: TQ 709610). Telephone: 01634 240228. Off the A228 Snodland bypass.

These reclaimed gravel pits cover 15 acres (6 hectares), and opportunities are provided for many forms of water sport including fishing, canoeing and windsurfing. Picnic areas, benches and a circular footpath create interest for all, with particular emphasis on access for the disabled.

Burham Downs Nature Reserve, Blue Bell Hill, Chatham (OS 178 and 188: TQ 738625). A quarter of a mile (400 metres) west of A229.

Interesting species of orchid and other plants are to be found in this small reserve of downland scrub and abandoned quarry which adjoins the Bluebell Hill Picnic Site.

Canterbury Cathedral.

Westgate Towers in St Peter's Street, Canterbury.

St Martin's, Canterbury, is the oldest parish church in England that is still in use.

Capstone Farm Country Park, Capstone Road, Chatham ME7 3JG (OS 178: TQ 780650). Telephone: 01634 812196. Off A2 2 miles (3 km) south of Chatham.

The park covers 280 acres (32 hectares) of open countryside including woodland and grassland. There are facilities for walking, fishing and horseriding. The lakeside is open all summer and most weekends in winter.

Clowes Wood, Blean (OS 179: TR 137630). Telephone: 01580 211044. 3 miles (5 km) east of A290 at Blean.

These 580 acres (235 hectares) of mixed woodland include a picnic area and a signposted walk of about 2 miles (3 km). Over fifty species of breeding bird have been recorded here, and there are fine views over the estuary of the Swale.

Cobtree Manor Park, off Forstal Road, Aylesford (OS 178 and 188: TQ 745584). Telephone: 01622 602188.

This 50 acre (20 hectare) open space was created out of the former Maidstone Zoo. Walks, nature trails and specialist tree identification leaflets are available. There are picnic tables and access for horseriding by permit.

Crab and Winkle Line Walk, Whitstable (OS 179).

A 7 mile (11 km) walk follows the route of the 'Crab and Winkle Line', which opened in 1830 as the first steam-powered passenger railway in the world. The line ran from Canterbury to Whitstable, part of the route running through a tunnel. On the inaugural trip one of the passengers walked back to Canterbury rather than go through the tunnel again! The Whitstable Improvement Trust (telephone: 01227 770060) has produced a leaflet guiding the visitor along the line, which closed in 1952.

Dartford Heath, Dartford (OS 177: TQ 520730). Off A2 near Dartford.

This 300 acre (121 hectare) area of heathland with light scrub is mainly flat and therefore ideal for long walks and other types of recreation. Some areas are managed whilst others are allowed to remain as fairly dense woodland. Wildlife abounds and there are many car parks dotted about the area, which is the second largest area of heathland in the county.

Dene Park, Shipbourne (OS 188: TQ 605511). Off A227 2 miles (3 km) north of Tonbridge.

The forest comprises 220 acres (89 hectares) of hardwood trees and offers some sheltered walks with pleasant views.

Dryhill Picnic Park, Riverhead (OS 188: TQ 499552). Off A25 1 mile (1.6 km) west of Riverhead.

This 22 acre (8.9 hectare) park was created from an ancient ragstone quarry. There are good walks, interesting old cliff faces and a picnic area.

Dungeness RSPB Nature Reserve, Boulderwall Farm, Dungeness Road, Lydd TN29 9PN (OS 189: TR 060199). Telephone: 01797 320588. 1 mile (1.6 km) south-east of Lydd.

Open all year except Tuesdays; closed Christmas and Boxing Day.

This specialist reserve is in the unique shingle habitat of Dungeness. There is an excellent visitor centre with hides, binocular hire and nature trail. The best times to visit are the spring and summer when the large seabird colony is supplemented by summer migrants, but in the winter there is a change in the species to be seen with the arrival of overwintering wildfowl.

Farningham Wood Nature Reserve, Farningham (OS 177: TQ 540680). Half a mile (800 metres) north of Farningham, off Button Street.

This varied habitat is managed by Sevenoaks District Council. A mixture of sand and chalk has produced an unusual combination of plant types. Heather and lily of the valley may be seen on the acid soils whilst the small-leaved lime can be found in only one other location in Kent. Another speciality is the Deptford pink, which grows on the edge of the woodland.

Folkestone Warren (OS 179 and 189: TR 240373). Half a mile (800 metres) south of A20 near Folkestone.

The Warren is an area of overgrown scrub at the base of the white chalk cliffs. It is of interest to geologists as it has long been subject to subsidence, and to naturalists for its migrant butterflies and birds. Fossils may be found along the beach, although the terrain is suited only to those wearing stout shoes.

Grove Ferry Picnic Site, Upstreet (OS 179: TR 237631). A quarter of a mile (400 metres) south of A28 at Upstreet.

There are 11 acres (4 hectares) of meadowland on the banks of the river Stour where day fishing tickets are available. The long walks available in the area make this an ideal centre from which to explore the countryside to the east of Canterbury.

Ham Street Woods National Nature Reserve, Hamstreet (OS 189: TR 005335). Half a mile (800 metres) north of Hamstreet, off B2067.

This reserve is made up of five small woods of the 'damp oak wood' type. Whilst the oak is the predominant tree, many others may be found here. The trees are coppiced to encourage the vigorous growth of new trees, whilst mature oaks are allowed to grow to a useful size. Over ninety species of bird have been recorded in the reserve, which is also rich in plant and insect life.

Hothfield Common Nature Reserve, Hothfield (OS 189: TQ 970456). Adjacent to A20, midway between Charing and Ashford.

Unique flora and fauna are to be found in this strange landscape. Until 1959 it was a common where villagers could graze animals and collect firewood and peat. In some areas the peat has formed bogs where the insectivorous plant sundew may be found. A wooden causeway allows visitors to view the plants without causing damage to the habitat. The neglected parts of the reserve are being enhanced by the clearance of the birch and bracken that quickly colonised the heathland, and a nature trail has been laid out.

Langdon Cliffs, Dover (OS 179: TR 335424). 1 mile (1.6 km) east of Castle Hill, Dover.

This is the best place from which to view the English Channel. Extensive clifftop paths lead to St Margaret's Bay whilst views over the busy Eastern Docks are of interest to those who do not wish to walk far. On a clear day the French coast may be seen whilst at dusk the numerous lighthouses on both sides of the Channel provide an entertaining spectacle.

Lullingstone Park, Kingfisher Bridge, Castle Road, Eynsford DA4 0JF (OS 177 and 188: TQ 508648). Telephone: 01322 865995. Off A225 1 mile (1.6 km) south of Eynsford.

Formerly the park of Lullingstone Castle (see page 73), this open space comprises 300 acres (120 hectares) of sloping land above the river Darent. There are walks in both woodland and parkland and a visitor centre from where guided walks start and other events are organised.

Manor Farm Country Park, West Malling (OS 178 and 188: TQ 678571). Off A228 half a mile (800 metres) south of West Malling church.

Although Douces Manor is now in commercial hands its 52 acre (21 hectare) park has been preserved along with a lake where interesting birdlife may be seen. The remains of an eighteenth-century icehouse can be seen nearby, whilst the nearby St Leonard's Tower forms a perfect backdrop. Information and nature trail leaflets are available.

The North Downs Way

This most interesting walk runs from Farnham in Surrey to Dover along the North Downs, the northern remnant of the Wealden dome of chalk. Because the countryside through which it runs is so variable the Way is ideal for walking in short sections. Part of the walk follows the course of the Pilgrims' Way, a traditional path that may date back to the Dark Ages.

The Way enters Kent at Westerham and passes Chevening House, a seventeenth-century building that is the official residence of the Foreign Secretary. The nearby church

A mural in Bromley commemorates H. G. Wells's association with the town.

The impressive clock-tower at Herne Bay was the tallest in the world when it was built in 1837.

Rochester Castle has one of the finest preserved Norman keeps in Britain.

is dedicated to St Botolph, a patron saint of travellers, indicating that the route here is ancient. At Otford the river Darent is crossed near the remains of the Archbishop's Palace (see page 26). The next village along the Downs is Kemsing, where a holy well associated with St Edith and a picturesque church draw many visitors. Next to the Bull Hotel in Wrotham is an interesting plaque recording the death of an officer during the Napoleonic Wars. He was shot by a deserter. From Wrotham the path follows the Pilgrims' Way and at Holly Hill extensive views across the Medway valley may be obtained.

The M2 bridge takes the path across the river Medway – quite an experience on a windy day – although an alternative route for those following the Way by car is via the city of Rochester. At Bluebell Hill the path runs adjacent to the picnic site and Burham Downs Nature Reserve and picnic site (see page 35) and passes close to some stone age monuments (see page 49).

At Lenham a large chalk cross is cut into the hillside as a village war memorial. The village of Charing has a picturesque group of medieval buildings, including the parish church and ruined Archbishop's Palace (viewable from the road only). Between Charing and Canterbury the most remote villages and countryside may be appreciated. Particularly beautiful is Eastwell Park with a ruined church (see page 64) which stands on the edge of a 40 acre (16 hectare) lake.

From Canterbury the path runs very close to the former Kent coalfields near Shepherdswell and through the glorious grounds of Waldershare Park to Dover. An alternative route from Canterbury runs via the Wye Downs.

Oare Marshes Nature Reserve, Oare (OS 178: TR 013648). 1 mile (1.6 km) north of Oare church.

This remarkable wetland habitat is the result of the construction of the sea wall following the severe floods of 1953. Until then this was a saltmarsh, but with the exclusion of the sea it has become freshwater land that can be used for grazing. Extensive views over the river Swale to the Isle of Sheppey may be gained from the sea wall. The reserve is most interesting in spring and autumn when vast numbers of waterbirds visit the site.

Pegwell Bay Country Park, Cliffs End, near Ramsgate (OS 179: TR 348639). Telephone: 01843 851137. On A256 1 mile (1.6 km) south of the junction with A253.

The river Stour reaches the sea at Pegwell Bay and this site hugs the coast with its rough grassland and extensive sea views. St Augustine landed here in AD 597 and a nearby monument commemorates this event. There is a public bird hide and leaflets are available from the Kent Wildlife Trust.

Queendown Warren Nature Reserve, Hartlip (OS 178 and 188: TQ 825629). 3 miles (5 km) north-east of the Kent County Showground.

During the middle ages this area of downland was used as a rabbit warren and sheep walk. The animals kept the grass short – and continue to do so. This grazing allows plants of a very specialised type to flourish, including some rare orchids. The very steep slope of the main warren is the reason why it has never been cultivated.

Riverside Country Park, Lower Twydall, Gillingham (OS 178: TQ 810681). Telephone: 01634 378987. 1 mile (1.6 km) east of Gillingham Strand.

Riverside Country Park, covering 120 acres (49 hectares), is ideal for walkers and birdwatchers. A picnic area, children's playground and visitor centre add to the attractions of the site.

Royal Military Canal Walk (OS 189). Hythe to Rye.

This newly waymarked walk through some of the least spoiled parts of Kent incorporates aspects of social, military and architectural history. A leaflet is available from tourist information centres. See also page 104.

Sandwich Bay Nature Reserve, Sandwich (OS 179: TR 350620). 2 miles (3 km) north of the clubhouse of Prince's Golf Club.

The reserve is made up of several different habitats including sand dunes, saltmarsh and rough grazing. Because the area is so exposed the plants tend to be dwarf or low lying. They include two uncommon species, the sea-holly and the sharp rush. Many migrant birds and insects land at the reserve on their inward journeys. The skyline is dominated by the massive cooling towers of the nearby power station. During the summer the song of the skylark and the smell of clover add to the magical atmosphere. The reserve may be reached by car via a toll road from Sandwich town centre followed by a long walk.

The Saxon Shore Way

This 140 mile (225 km) long walk is a fine way to explore the maritime history of the county. Not only does it link the Roman forts constructed to defend the area from Saxon invaders, but it also encompasses many later towns, each of which displays a different character. Because the route runs along the coast this is an ideal walk to tackle in sections from a central base, avoiding the inconvenience of having to find new accommodation along the route.

The walk starts at Gravesend and crosses the flat marshes so well described by Dickens in *Great Expectations* (see page 106). It runs through several sleepy villages, including Cliffe and Upnor, which looks like it has come straight from a Hollywood film set. After passing through the Medway Towns the route runs along the Medway estuary and through the charming village of Lower Halstow, where the river laps the churchyard wall. It also passes the site of an isolation hospital erected on a remote hill in 1801 not far from the modern Kingsferry Bridge, the only link between the Isle of Sheppey and mainland. From there its course is along the river Swale, through Sittingbourne and the Oare Marshes and South Swale nature reserves to the town of Whitstable, famous for its oysters (see page 34). After Herne Bay, the walker turns inland at Reculver (see page 50) along what was the former shoreline to Richborough (see page 51), which is just outside the ancient town of Sandwich. Although the path does not go into the town centre its skyline punctuates the walk until the beach is reached again at Sandwich Bay. As the path runs through Deal the cliffs start to rise again

until at Dover they are at their highest, with fine views across to France. At Hythe the path again keeps to the former coastline, which is some way inland, to Lympne Castle (see page 56). A little further on the path runs through the Isle of Oxney, now a hill rising from the marsh, where there is an unusual Roman altar in the parish church, before it crosses the county boundary into Sussex to end at Rye a few miles to the west.

Sevenoaks Wildfowl Reserve, Bradbourne Vale Road, Sevenoaks (OS 188: TQ 520570). Telephone: 01732 456407.

Within the 135 acres (55 hectares) there are ponds, reed beds and woodland. A display at the visitor centre explains the creation of the reserve and the wildlife which may be found. As well as three viewing hides there are a nature trail, picnic area and refreshment kiosk.

Shorne Wood Country Park, Brewers Road, Shorne, Gravesend DA12 2HX (OS 177 and 178: TQ 680696). Telephone: 01474 823800. Off A2 between Gravesend and Rochester.

This country park is a multi-recreational centre with woodland, ponds, meadows and heathland suitable for many types of countryside recreation including walking, picnics, orienteering, fishing and riding. A visitor centre is open during the summer and leaflets and audio-guides are available.

South Swale Nature Reserve, Graveney (OS 178 and 179: TR 040650). Half a mile (800 metres) east of Ye Olde Sportsman public house.

This reserve comprises mudflats and beach on the south side of the Swale estuary. It is bordered by the Saxon Shore Way, from which the whole reserve may be viewed. Together, the Oare Marshes and South Swale reserves provide protection for a large portion of the Swale riverbank.

Stodmarsh National Nature Reserve, Stodmarsh (OS 179: TR 221610). Telephone: 01227 728382. Half a mile (800 metres) north of Stodmarsh church.

The reserve was established in 1968 to protect a marshland habitat in the valley of

The tower of St George's church in the centre of Gravesend.

The Priory gardens and Bromley Museum in Orpington.

The New College of Cobham is a group of almshouses and Great Hall built behind the parish church.

The North Downs Way passes through Trosley Country Park.

the Great Stour river. Many of the lakes were formed by subsidence resulting from nearby coal mining. The reserve is particularly interesting as a wintering place for many types of waterbird, whilst in the summer the reed beds provide nesting places for many different species. The public path runs along a flood defence wall from the village of Stodmarsh to Grove Ferry, giving excellent views over each different habitat.

Teston Bridge Picnic Site, Teston (OS 188: TQ 708532). On A26 3 miles (5 km) south of Maidstone.

These 24 acres (10 hectares) of watermeadows are ideal for short strolls along the river Medway, where barges used to be towed. The mill house opposite and the manor house on the hill above dominate the landscape, whilst the medieval bridge is of great historic interest.

Toys Hill (OS 188: TQ 470515). Off A25 2½ miles (4 km) south of Brasted.

200 acres (80 hectares) of woodland, replanted after the storm of 1987, provide walks of many different types. Leaflets are available from the National Trust at Emmetts Garden and Chartwell.

Trosley Country Park, Waterlow Road, Meopham, Gravesend DA13 0SG (OS 177 and 188: TQ 637612). Telephone: 01732 823570. Off A227 3 miles (5 km) south of Meopham church.

In the nineteenth century this was the park of Trosley Towers, home of the Waterlow family. After the demolition of the house the estate went wild until the establishment of a country park. The rhododendrons and azaleas that have grown up in the woodland are a major feature. There are miles of paths for walkers of all abilities and nature-trail and information leaflets are available.

Tunbridge Wells Common, Tunbridge Wells (OS 188: TQ 575390). In the centre of Tunbridge Wells.

Tunbridge Wells is unique in Kent in having large undeveloped areas in its heart. The common comprises 160 acres (65 hectares) of ancient woodland that has changed little since Queen Henrietta Maria camped there in 1630 whilst taking the waters. Apart from woodland and open spaces there are some dramatic outcrops of sandstone that provide picturesque locations for artists and playgrounds for children.

The Wealdway Path

The Wealdway was conceived by the Ramblers Association in 1970. It runs from Gravesend to Eastbourne. In Kent it crosses the arable areas of the North Downs, the orchards of the Medway valley and the sandstone ridge north of Tonbridge. Unlike the Saxon Shore Way, it does not lend itself to exploration from a fixed centre, although sections may be walked in turn.

The area on top of the North Downs escarpment is little populated. This is partly the result of the Black Death, which ravaged the countryside here in 1348. Many villages were destroyed altogether and the paths runs through several, including Luddesdowne, where a glimpse may be had of one of the oldest inhabited houses in England, Luddesdowne Court, as the path runs past its front gate. A little further on the deserted village of Dode is evidence of the power of the Black Death. Its restored church may be visited by appointment (see page 64). The path drops down the escarpment near Trottiscliffe, running through the Coldrum Stones (page 49), and over grassy heathland near Mereworth. The village of West Peckham, with its delightful church (see page 68), green and pub, makes a convenient stopping place. Between West Peckham and Tonbridge the Wealdway runs through pleasant agricultural lands with orchards and hop gardens. At Tonbridge the path runs through the castle grounds (see page 57) and within a few minutes is back in open countryside. The final Kent section climbs the sandstone ridge and runs through the charming village of Bidborough, which has an interesting church clock whose pendulum swings under the tower. It then passes through Speldhurst (see page 68) until the Sussex border is reached near Stone Cross. The path then continues a further 40 miles (64 km) to Eastbourne.

West Wood, Lyminge (OS 179 and 189: TR 140440). Off B2068, 8 miles (13 km) south of Canterbury.

This dense woodland site in an area of Kent that is often missed by the visitor has a 2½ mile (4 km) walk.

Wye National Nature Reserve, Wye (OS 179 and 189: TR 078453). 2 miles (3 km) east of Wye church.

This chalk downland provides a specialised habitat that must be managed to prevent it becoming overgrown with scrub. Formerly the area was intensively farmed and the remains of ancient field boundaries may still be seen. The open grassland is home to many species of butterfly and orchid. During summer care should be taken as adders are common. There is a nature trail and a visitor centre, where further information may be obtained.

Yockletts Bank Nature Reserve, Waltham (OS 179 and 189: TR 125478). 1 mile (1.6 km) south-west of Waltham church.

This 60 acre (24 hectare) reserve is rich in woodland flora, including the lady orchid, bluebell and primrose. Many birds breed here and several species of mammal have been recorded amongst the ash, hornbeam and hazel trees.

Minster Abbey in Thanet is occupied by Roman Catholic nuns, who have restored the building.

The Coldrum Stones are the remains of a long barrow near Trottiscliffe.

4
Sites of archaeological interest

The Coldrum Stones, Trottiscliffe (OS 177, 178 and 188: TQ 654607). Half a mile (800 metres) east of Trottiscliffe church.
Open at all times.

This is a small chambered long barrow dating from the neolithic period and forming part of a group of such structures on the western side of the Medway valley. It comprises a rectangle of sarsen stones with a burial chamber at the eastern end. This was excavated in the nineteenth century and produced the remains of at least twenty-two people. These were later buried in Meopham churchyard, leading the rector of Trottiscliffe to ask the priest at Meopham what had happened to his oldest parishioners! The site was badly damaged by quarrying but is now protected and offers fine views across this part of the valley.

The Countless Stones, Aylesford (OS 178 and 188: TQ 745604). 2 miles (3 km) north of Maidstone off A229.
Open at all times.

The Countless Stones (or Little Kit's Coty) stand ¹/₄ mile (400 metres) south of Kit's Coty House (see below). They were a chambered tomb similar to Coldrum, surviving until treasure seekers dug under it in the eighteenth century. Today there is just a pile of stones standing isolated in a field. The name derives from a local tradition that the Devil tries to stop anyone counting them. One day, so legend says, a baker put a loaf of bread on each one as he counted it, but when he finished he discovered that the Devil had been eating the loaves behind his back!

Crofton Roman Villa, Crofton Road, Orpington. Telephone: 01689 873826.
Open April to October, Wednesdays, Fridays

and Sunday afternoons.

Under a purpose-built viewing building are the remains of ten of the rooms of the villa house, with interpretation panels and details of the excavations by the Kent Archaeological Rescue Unit.

Kit's Coty House, Aylesford (OS 178 and 188: TQ 745608). 2 miles (3 km) north of Maidstone off A229.
Open at all times.

The most impressive prehistoric burial chamber in the county takes its name from a shepherd called Kit who used the stones for shelter in the seventeenth century. It was originally a long barrow, with the surviving stones forming a false doorway at the east end. The doorway may have been a showpiece against which ceremonies might have been conducted. It had a solid earthen mound behind it. Burials were probably placed beneath the mound, which has been removed by ploughing, leaving the stones standing alone. They stand over 8 feet (2.4 metres) high and consist of three upright stones with one horizontal stone lying on top of them. Samuel Pepys visited this site in 1669 and 'was mightily pleased with the sight of it'. There are wide-ranging views from this side of the escarpment. The stones are now protected by railings and are reached by a very steep path, unsuitable for those with mobility problems.

Lullingstone Roman Villa, Lullingstone Lane, Eynsford, Dartford DA4 0JA (OS 177: TQ 529651). Telephone: 01322 863467. Half a mile (800 metres) south of Eynsford village.
Open daily.

In the middle of the eighteenth century estate workmen erecting a park fence for Lullingstone Castle (see page 73) discovered

This fourth-century Roman mosaic at Lullingstone Roman Villa depicts the legend of Europa and the bull.

a Roman mosaic floor a few feet below ground level. Two hundred years later systematic excavation took place to reveal one of the best preserved villas in England, inhabited for nearly three centuries. The first buildings were constructed about AD 80. During the period of its occupation its owners converted to Christianity and built a chapel. This makes Lullingstone one of the earliest Christian sites in Britain. After excavation the major part of the building was enclosed under a permanent roof so that the splendid mosaic floors can be observed. The best ones symbolise the Seasons and the Abduction of Europa and date from the last quarter of the fourth century.

Oldbury Hillfort, Ightham (OS 188: TQ 581561). Half a mile (800 metres) north of A25 at Ightham village.
Open at all times.

This delightful area of mixed woodland incorporates a large prehistoric earthwork of 123 acres (50 hectares). The bank and ditch system of defence was a particularly effective method when used on a hilltop such as this. Thousands of trees would have been felled to provide timber for a massive palisade at the time of its construction at the end of the second century BC. Following Caesar's invasions of 55 and 54 BC the ditches were recut and the defences extended. In the same area is an interesting group of stone age rock shelters (on private land and not accessible).

Reculver Roman Fort and Saxon Church, Reculver (OS 179: TR 228694). On the coast east of Herne Bay.
Open at all times.

The fort of *Regulbium* was constructed to protect the Wantsum Channel in the early part of the third century AD. Today the Wantsum is silted up and Reculver has grown into a caravan park. Whilst the Roman harbour has been destroyed, parts of the fort remain on the clifftop, which is now protected from erosion. Tradition says that King Ethelbert was converted to Christianity there in the early seventh century and erected a cross to commemorate this event. In AD 669 Egbert founded a small church over the site of the cross and this building grew into a monastery. The foundations of this church may still be seen although only the later west towers are still standing. The church was demolished in the early nineteenth century because the vicar thought the position too exposed. Two of the Saxon pillars are now in the crypt of Canterbury Cathedral. The twin towers were allowed to remain as an aid to navigation. Today the monument is preserved by English Heritage and is known locally as 'Reculver Towers'.

Richborough Castle (Roman fort), Richborough, Sandwich CT13 9JW (OS 179: TR 324602). Telephone: 01304 612013. Off A257 north of Sandwich.
Open daily during the summer.

This is where the Claudian invasion of Britain probably began in AD 43. The area was first defended with double ditches which were soon filled in and covered by granaries and storerooms. After AD 85 the Romans erected a triumphal arch, faced with white marble and statues, which formed the official entrance to Britain, at the beginning of Watling Street, the main road to London. The base of this gateway survives and fragments of its structure may be seen in the site museum. Two hundred years after the erection of the arch the area was fortified by flint walls, which still dominate the site today. They were built about AD 286 by Carausius, the Emperor in Britain, at a time when Saxon raiders first became active along the Channel coast. Much of the fort wall stands to its original height of 25 feet (7.6 metres). The hollow of an amphitheatre can still be seen some half a mile (800 metres) south of the fort.

Roman Museum, Butchery Lane, Canterbury (OS 179: TR 150577). Telephone: 01227 785575.
Open all year, Monday to Saturday; also Sundays in summer.

Following the redevelopment of the area in the 1980s the opportunity was taken to build a specialist museum around an outstanding Roman pavement beneath the shopping centre.

Reculver Towers are the remains of a Saxon church founded on the site of a Roman fort.

There are displays about Roman Canterbury using artefacts discovered throughout the city, some hands-on exhibits for children and an audio-visual display. The pavement, however, is the main attraction. It is hard to imagine how this small part of a much larger complex of buildings has survived in the centre of such a densely populated commercial site.

Roman Painted House, New Street, Dover CT17 9AJ (OS 179: TR 318415). Telephone: 01304 203279.
Open April to October, daily except Mondays (but open seven days a week in July and August).
The Roman House was discovered in 1971. It originally stood just outside a third-century Roman fort. The house is built of flint and brick and probably dates from about AD 200. The larger rooms have a hypocaust system and all the floors were of red mortar. The walls of the two main rooms have been preserved up to a height of about 6 feet (2 metres) and these are plastered and painted with high quality pictures. There is no comparable site outside Italy. The main form of decoration consists of rectangular panels separated by painted columns. The site has been preserved under a permanent building and provides a unique insight into the development of a town house in the third century. Parts of the massive stone wall of the fort, built about AD 270, can be seen and many finds are on show.

Roman Pharos, Dover (OS 179: TR 326418). Telephone: 01304 201628. Within the grounds of Dover Castle.
Open daily throughout the year.
Standing next to the late Saxon church of St Mary, this rare survival served to guide Roman ships into the harbour below. Until the nineteenth century it had a twin standing on the Western Heights, engulfed but at least partially conserved by the Napoleonic fortifications. Both structures would have shown a light at night and smoke during the day, so that ships could set a middle course into the harbour. For this reason these are not so much lighthouses, which warn ships off the coast, as beacons to draw them in, although the surviving structure has long been known as

The Roman Pharos, or lighthouse, stands in the grounds of Dover Castle.

'the Roman lighthouse'. The lower 43 feet (13 metres) of the Pharos dates from the first century AD and is built of a flint rubble core, bonded with courses of tile and faced with tufa ashlar. The upper part is medieval and became a freestanding bell-tower when the church was built about 1000.

St Leonard's Tower, West Malling (OS 178 and 188: TQ 675570).
Open at all times.
It is generally accepted that this unusually well-preserved tower of about 1100 was built as a defensive structure to protect the nearby Malling Abbey and its important agricultural land. The lower stages of the tower are largely built of tufa, with some local ragstone. There was originally a chapel there, which gave the tower its name; one surviving wall of this may be seen to the south of the tower. On the opposite side of the road is Manor Farm Country Park (see page 39).

5
Castles and other defences

Cooling Castle, Cooling, near Rochester.
Not open to the public but may be viewed from the road.

Although it is not open to the public, Cooling Castle is close enough to the road to be worth a visit. Its round-towered gateway dates from the 1380s and dominates the Thames estuary beyond. In 1554 the castle was besieged by a force led by Sir Thomas Wyatt of Allington Castle, who was protesting against the marriage of Queen Mary I to Philip of Spain. Wyatt's brother-in-law, Lord Cobham, lived at Cooling Castle at that time, but with only eight men to defend it the castle held out for only six hours. As a punishment for allowing the rebels to capture his castle, Lord Cobham and his family were imprisoned in the Tower of London, where Thomas Cobham carved his name on the wall of the Beauchamp Tower. Cooling Castle was left to fall down, and now forms a picturesque ruin. A modern house stands within the walls.

Deal Castle, Victoria Road, Deal CT14 7BA. Telephone: 01304 372762.
Open daily, except Mondays and Tuesdays in winter.

Henry VIII built four castles in Kent during the period 1539-40 to strengthen his precarious defences along the English Channel and to protect the Downes anchorage. Two survive more or less intact, at Deal and Walmer. Deal Castle consists of a three-tiered building. Clustered around the central keep at a lower level are six semicircular bastions; at a still lower level is the outer curtain from which project another six bastions. From the air it looks rather like a flat wedding cake. The whole castle hugs the ground and is surrounded by a wide dry moat. It is primarily a functional structure, built for carrying artillery, with storerooms, passages and gun emplacements. Accommodation for the gunners and offices were provided in the keep but were of secondary concern in the castle's design. Even though the castle has excellent views out to sea it saw little action. A tape tour is available which takes visitors to all levels of the building.

Dover Castle, Dover CT16 1HU. Telephone: 01304 201628.
Open daily.

The eastern cliff at Dover was crowned with an iron age hillfort. Within that enclosure the Romans built a beacon tower (see page 52) and the Saxons a church. The present castle, also within the earlier defences, was started during the reign of Henry II (1154-89). The English barons, unhappy with the rule of King John, invited Prince Louis of France to seize the English throne and in 1216 he tried to capture Dover Castle. With the premature death of King John at Newark their cause was lost and Louis went back to France. The constableship of Dover Castle has long been associated with the title Lord Warden of the Cinque Ports and is a position of great prestige. Beneath the castle are some remarkable tunnels dating from the thirteenth and nineteenth centuries and from the Second World War. The keep has been altered to some extent to take larger guns, particularly during the Napoleonic period, but it remains in an excellent state of preservation. Fine views over the town and harbour may be obtained from the roof. More of the castle is now being opened to the public and one of the most popular areas is the Secret Wartime Tunnels, a series of underground works used during the Second World War, when Dover was very much in the front line of defence.

Dymchurch Martello Tower, High Street, Dymchurch, Romney Marsh. Telephone: 01303 873684.
Open: May to July, weekends; August, daily.

Martello towers were built in the early nine-

Deal Castle was one of four Henrican castles built in Kent.

teenth century when there was a threat of a French invasion. There were originally seventy-four towers between Folkestone and Seaford, intended to strengthen key strategic points such as sluices in the Royal Military Canal; the tower at Dymchurch was number 24. Each was a single tower with a gun emplacement able to concentrate fire on ships at sea and repel enemy landings. The Dymchurch tower contains displays showing the development of these unusual defences.

Eynsford Castle, Eynsford.
Open at all times.

This unusual small Norman castle in the Darent valley was built in about 1100 of flint rubble and consisted of a curtain wall containing a freestanding hall. The hall was probably abandoned in the fourteenth century and the surrounding walls subsequently provided shelter for a variety of purposes including, in the eighteenth century, kennels for hunting dogs. The curtain wall still stands for most of its original length and the whole site gives a good idea of the domestic arrangements of the medieval period.

Fort Amherst, Dock Road, Chatham ME4 4UB. Telephone: 01634 847747.
Open daily.

Fort Amherst was built in 1756 to protect the naval dockyard at Chatham from landward attack. The fortifications cover 14 acres (5.7 hectares) and comprise massive ditches, numerous gun positions, huge bastions and a network of underground passages. It is the best surviving Georgian fortress in Britain, taking its present form between 1802 and 1811. The gatehouse has been restored to its original appearance; on the ground floor is a museum while on the upper floor the living conditions of Wellington's soldiers have been recreated in a barrack room. During the summer scenes from the fort's history are often recreated and throughout the year special events add to the popularity of this attraction where 'living history' may be studied to great advantage.

The Grand Shaft Staircase, Snargate Street, Dover. Telephone: 01304 201066.
Open July and August only, daily except Mondays.

In the early nineteenth century the cliffs to the west of Dover were used as an enormous garrison. The top of the cliffs contained a huge fort, but a means of easy access was required to get men to and from the harbour below. The Grand Shaft was the answer. It is a well-shaft around which three separate and non-communicating staircases were constructed, each being lit from the well-shaft. According to tradition each staircase was allocated to a different rank of soldier! It is an extraordinary building that deserves to be better known, despite its limited opening period.

Hever Castle, Hever, Edenbridge TN8 7NG. Telephone: 01732 865224.
Open March to November, daily.

Hever Castle has a superb setting but the 'Tudor village' that today forms the backdrop to the thirteenth-century moated castle was built by the Astor family in 1906. The vast Italianate gardens were created for the first Lord Astor, who employed one thousand workmen for four years at the start of the twentieth century.

Hever is best-known for its associations with Anne Boleyn, second wife of Henry VIII. It was her family home until her marriage and Henry must have visited her there many times. Her father, Thomas, is buried in the nearby church. After his death the estate passed to the Crown and was leased to royal favourites. It soon entered obscurity and was a mere farmhouse when William Waldorf Astor purchased it in 1903. His 'Tudor village' was designed as guest accommodation for those attending his house parties and may today be hired for functions.

The castle is furnished with period furniture and has a 'lived-in' atmosphere, and there are historical displays highlighting the Tudor period. The gardens run down to the 35 acre (14 hectare) lake and are dotted with ancient

Leeds Castle has been called 'the most beautiful castle in the world'.

marbles. There is an excellent yew maze. A herbaceous border 120 yards (110 metres) long and a unique water maze were introduced in 1997.

Leeds Castle, Leeds, Maidstone ME17 1DL. Telephone: 01622 765400.
Open daily.

Today Leeds Castle is one of England's top tourist attractions. In the ninth century a wooden castle was built here on an island in the valley of the river Len. After the Norman Conquest it passed through several hands until Edward I gave it to his wife, Eleanor of Castile, and so began the long tradition of Leeds being a 'Queen's castle'. After Henry VIII's death it was given to Sir Antony St Leger as a reward for services rendered to the Crown and it passed out of royal hands. In the seventeenth century it was the home of an old Kent family, the Culpepers, and it passed from them to the Fairfaxes and the Wykeham-Martins. During the 1920s and 1930s the castle was restored by the Honourable Lady Baillie, who worked hard to recreate what is now called 'the most beautiful castle in the world'. In addition to the furnished rooms there is an unusual museum of dog collars, a woodland garden, grotto and maze and a modern aviary. The main visitor route to the castle consists of a substantial walk though the wildfowl and water gardens, although transport is available for those with mobility problems. The castle offers several major events each year including open-air concerts and firework displays.

Lympne Castle, Lympne, near Hythe CT21 4LQ. Telephone: 01303 267571.
Open June to mid September, Mondays to Thursdays.

The remains of the Roman *Portus Lemanis* lie at the base of the cliff, from which a watch-tower once commanded wide views over the sea and provided warning of the approach of Saxons, Danes and Normans. Domesday Book recorded that the tower had become a parsonage house for seven Saxon priests, but the Normans dispossessed them and Lanfranc, Archbishop of Canterbury, built a castle there for his archdeacons. As feudal lords the archdeacons had to supply troops for the king and maintain a secure stronghold. In 1420 the west tower was built to house the garrison. The Norman tower continued to be used as a lookout by the army whenever invasion was threatened, up to the Second World War. Today the castle is a private home, with superb views over Romney Marsh, and is a popular location for civil wedding ceremonies.

New Tavern Fort, Fort Gardens, Gravesend. Telephone: 01474 323415.
Fort Gardens and emplacements open all year. Magazines open May to September, weekends and bank holidays.

In 1780 an earthwork battery for fifteen heavy cannon was built here to guard against the threat of French attack from the Thames. The brick emplacements were added in 1872 by General Gordon while he was commanding Royal Engineer of the Thames District. Many of these have now been rearmed. There was further improvement before the First World War when the fort formed part of the defence of London, as it did also during the Second World War. Traces of the original fort remain in the loopholed defence walls and the ditch defence. Restoration began in 1975. Beneath the fort is the fascinating Victorian underground magazine of sixteen chambers, some restocked as shell and cartridge rooms, others with fitted shelters from the Second World War. Restoration work continues here and also on the later magazine of 1904, to which public access is limited.

Rochester Castle, Rochester ME1 1SW. Telephone: 01634 402276.
Open daily.

The first castle was built here at the time of the Norman Conquest, although the present keep dates from 1127. At that time it was held by the Archbishop of Canterbury and in 1215 it was used by the rebel barons to stop King John marching on London. After a siege of two months the castle fell and the present south-eastern corner had to be rebuilt. It is round, in the style of the time, whilst the earlier towers are square. After several later sieges the castle declined in importance and only narrowly escaped total demolition in the eighteenth century. It remains one of the finest preserved Norman keeps in Britain, even though it is only a shell. The well, in the centre partition of the keep, was ingeniously constructed to allow access from all floors, and when the visitor reaches the battlements he can understand why this was a necessity.

Sandgate Castle, Castle Road, Sandgate, Folkestone CT20 3AG. Telephone: 01303 221881.
Open by appointment only.
Sandgate Castle was one of the castles Henry VIII built in 1539-40 to protect the Channel coast against a possible French invasion. It had three bastions and a central keep. Both Henry and Elizabeth I stayed here. 250 years later it was refortified as a Napoleonic fortification and became a glorified martello tower. This necessitated clearing away many

Scotney Castle and its moat form the centrepiece of a lovely garden.

of the Tudor buildings to form a continuous promenade around the central tower. The garrison was withdrawn in 1881 and the castle has been in private hands since 1893, although it was used as an air-raid shelter in the Second World War. Massive coastal erosion had caused severe damage but its owners began restoration in the late 1970s. The castle is open to groups by appointment.

Scotney Castle, Lamberhurst TN3 8JN. Telephone: 01892 890651.
Garden open March to November. Castle ruins open May to September, except Mondays and Tuesdays.
The medieval Scotney Castle stands in the valley of the river Bewl, surrounded by delightful gardens. It was built in 1378 by Roger de Ashburnham as a fortified manor house. A moat was formed by damming the river and creating two islands. For three hundred years it was the home of the Darrells, a Catholic family, who harboured a Jesuit priest here at times of religious persecution. In 1837 the castle was partly demolished to create a picturesque ruin visible from the new house built on the hill above. The splendid gardens were laid out to make the most of the steeply sloping grounds and feature a thatched icehouse. The nineteenth-century house is not open to the public.

Tonbridge Castle, Castle Street, Tonbridge TN9 1BG. Telephone: 01732 770929.
Open daily.
The castle stands on the banks of the river Medway in the centre of Tonbridge. It was built as a motte and bailey castle by Richard Fitzgilbert (or de Clare as he often styled himself), making use of an earlier earthwork. This motte is still the most important visual feature, rising to a height of 60 feet (18 metres) and giving views over the upper Medway valley. In the thirteenth century the curtain walls and great stone gatehouse were added. After Gilbert de Clare was killed at the battle of Bannockburn in 1314 the castle passed through several families in quick succession. In the Civil War it was successfully held by the Parliamentarians, but by this time it was little more than a ruin. In the eighteenth century a mansion house was built in the bailey

and this now houses an award-winning tourist information centre and council offices. The gatehouse has a superb display brought to life by tableaux and an audio guide, describing life in the castle in the thirteenth century.

Upnor Castle, High Street, Upper Upnor, Rochester ME2 4XG. Telephone: 01634 718742. *Open April to September, daily.*

Queen Elizabeth I began Upnor Castle in 1559 to protect Chatham anchorage. The building was completed in 1567 under the supervision of Richard Watts, who secured stone from Rochester Castle to help the work along. Upnor Castle is a rectangular building with an angle bastion jutting out into the river, flanked by two D-shaped towers. Although it is very small it should have provided excellent protection of the river, yet when the Dutch sailed up the Medway in 1667 they were able to burn ships at anchor despite being subjected to heavy fire from Upnor. The following year it was relegated to use as a store, as new fortifications built in response to the Dutch raid superseded it. To-

day it offers a good display about the so called 'Battle of the Medway' and affords good views over the bustling river.

Walmer Castle, Kingsdown Road, Walmer, Deal CT14 7LJ. Telephone: 01304 364288. *Open April to October, daily; limited opening in winter.*

Walmer Castle was built by Henry VIII in 1539-40 to complement his other castles along the coast. It is in the same style as Deal Castle, having four bastions instead of six, and since 1708 it has been the official residence of the Lord Warden of the Cinque Ports. When the Duke of Wellington was Lord Warden Walmer Castle was his preferred country residence and it was here that he died. His room has been kept much as it was then and there are interesting displays of items relating to him. While Deal Castle remains a fort, Walmer has been adapted as a comfortable residence. The gardens at Walmer are small but charming, with massive yew hedges and pine trees sheltering the area from the exposed coastline.

The gatehouse of Tonbridge Castle was built in the thirteenth century.

6
Churches, chapels and monastic remains

The majority of the churches described here are open daily but before making a long journey it is advisable to telephone the incumbent, whose name and telephone number may be obtained from *Crockford's Clerical Directory*, which is available in most reference libraries.

Appledore: St Peter and St Paul. (On B2080 south-east of Tenterden.)

A rather misshapen church as a result of French raids in the fourteenth century, this picturesque building stands at the end of Appledore's main street. An outstanding feature is the stained glass of the nineteenth and twentieth centuries. One window shows the neighbouring church of St Thomas à Becket at Fairfield surrounded by sheep; it commemorates a grazier who spent his working life on the nearby marshes. Another has an electricity pylon in the bottom left-hand corner – a better way of saying 'twentieth century' than simply adding the date.

Ash next Wrotham: St Peter and St Paul. (South of Gravesend, west of A227.)

This large church in a very quiet location high on the Downs shows major work of the fourteenth century, repaired with brick in the eighteenth century and sympathetically restored in the early twentieth century by the noted architect Sir T. G. Jackson. The Hodsalls, a prominent local family, are well represented by monuments in the north chancel chapel. Much light floods into this typical country church, where the work done to the building reflected periods of agricultural prosperity.

Aylesford Priory, Aylesford. Telephone: 01622 717272. North-west of Maidstone, north of A20.
Open daily.

The priory was founded in 1242 by a few hermits who came here from the slopes of Mount Carmel in the entourage of Richard de Grey, lord of the manor of Aylesford. A local man, Simon Stock, encouraged them to give up their solitary life and become a community, and he later became their first prior. His relics may still be seen in a purpose-built chapel. Nothing remains of the medieval church, although its plan is picked out in the pavement, but the guests' hall and the domestic buildings of the courtyard remain. At the Dissolution of the Monasteries the church was destroyed and the cloisters were con-

Aylesford Priory has been restored by the Order of Carmelites for pilgrimage and worship.

Barfrestone church has elaborate Norman carvings.

verted into a mansion, whose owners played an important part in the life of the village (see page 9). After a fire in 1930 the property was bought by the Carmelite Order, who returned to their first English home. All but one of the chapels has been built by them subsequently and the priory is once more a popular place of pilgrimage.

Barfrestone: St Nicholas. (South-east of Canterbury, between A2 and A256.)

This Norman church was probably founded by Hugo de Port, a sub-constable of Dover Castle, but that alone does not explain the wonderful carvings that make Barfrestone one of the most important twelfth-century churches in England. Our Lord in Glory is depicted on the stone tympanum of the south doorway. Two later mass dials are scratched on the stone frames. All around the church are small heads of spiritual and mythical subjects, whilst the interior is equally elaborate. Unfortunately the interior work has been damaged, but there is much of interest and the setting alone is worth the visit.

Betteshanger: St Mary. (West of Deal, east of A256.)

A great favourite amongst those who seek out good examples of nineteenth-century architecture, Betteshanger church was built in 1853 to the designs of Anthony Salvin. A few objects, including an eighteenth-century monument by Peter Scheemakers, survive from the previous building. However, it is the Victorian work that dominates. This includes four good stained glass windows by Charles Eamer Kempe, dating from 1891, and an imposing Byzantine porch. The setting, in the grounds of Betteshanger Place, is a great bonus.

Birchington: All Saints. (West of Margate, on A28.)

Dante Gabriel Rossetti, who died in Birchington, is buried in the churchyard. His grave is to the south of the church, near the main pathway, and was designed by Ford Madox Brown, one of his Pre-Raphaelite contemporaries. The church is a large and impressive structure dating in the main from the fourteenth century and completely dominates the village centre. The font, which retains marks of its original lock, is an excellent example of thirteenth-century work. In the north chapel, the traditional burial place of the owners of Quex House (see page 76), are some good monuments; especially notable is the 'six-bust' monument of 1651.

Birling: All Saints. (North of West Malling, west of A228.)

This is very much an estate church which mirrors the fortunes of the lords of the manor. It stands on a small hill in the centre of the village, surrounded by an interesting churchyard, for which a 'trail' leaflet has been produced. Inside the church the Nevill family dominates: memorials to them abound, including the cast-iron cover to their family vault in front of the altar. In the nineteenth century the family was especially generous and restored the church, adding their own handiwork as well as commissioning others. The font cover, an enormous structure of carved woodwork, was carved by three female members of the family and is a real *tour de force*.

Boxley: St Mary and All Saints. (North of Maidstone, between A229 and A249.)

To many the setting of Boxley church is typical of Kent: a long rectangular green with a pub at one end and the church at the other. Yet Boxley is an unusual church in that it is two churches in one. A two-cell Norman church was replaced in the fourteenth century by a completely new church which was added to the east of the original. The visitor enters what was the nave of the Norman church, then steps into the former chancel, which is now the tower, following which the nave of the fourteenth-century church is discovered! This allows us to contrast the work of the two periods in a way that is impossible elsewhere. Alfred, Lord Tennyson, worshipped at Boxley and his poem 'The Brook' describes the countryside nearby.

Brabourne: St Mary. (East of Ashford, north of A20.)

This is a sizeable Norman church which displays some good examples of medieval art. The most important feature is the north chancel window, which dates from the twelfth century and is the oldest stained glass still in its original position in any Kent parish church. There is also a thirteenth-century heart shrine, a feature popular in the middle ages when because of transport difficulties the complete bodies of people who died abroad could not be brought home for burial. The interior of the church is tall and sombre and full of atmosphere.

Brenchley: All Saints. (North-east of Tunbridge Wells, east of B2160.)

Brenchley is a picturesque village, complemented by a wonderful church. The base of the rood screen, which survives *in situ*, dates from 1536 – making it one of the last to be built in Kent before the Reformation. The light interior is welcoming and well cared for and some of the twentieth-century stained glass is by Robert Anning Bell.

Brookland: St Augustine. (West of New Romney, on A259.)

The marshy land caused many problems for church builders in this part of Kent and at Brookland they were forced to put the bells in a cage on the ground rather than build a heavy tower. This cage was later encased in weatherboarding to protect not just the bells but the bellringers as well. It is often described as looking like a candle snuffer, with each of its three stages set over the top of the one below it. Inside the church is further evidence of the unstable ground, for the arcades to north and south bow outwards considerably. There is an unusual Norman lead font, cast with the Labours of the Months and the Signs of the Zodiac, and a fine wall-painting depicts the murder of Thomas à Becket.

Canterbury: Cathedral Church of Christ. Telephone: 01227 762862.
Open daily.

The view of Canterbury Cathedral, as seen by approaching visitors, is of a great building, perfect in shape and architecture. From a distance there seem to be none of the homely qualities that are so common in English cathedrals. As the mother church of the Anglican Communion, Canterbury fulfils its role very well, but this is with the loss of some character, for the building overwhelms.

Its awe-inspiring nave is one of the highlights of English Perpendicular architecture, dating from 1378-1405. Like many other parts of the building the grandeur is misleading, for it is built on the site of its Norman and Saxon predecessors. The master mason for the work was probably Henry Yevele, who had completed the nave of Westminster Abbey a few years earlier. From the outside the nave and chancel have the same roofline, but because the east end is built upon the Norman crypt the nave is much taller. The north-west transept, where Thomas à Becket was murdered in December 1170, is relatively empty except for a small modern altar to mark the place of martyrdom. A doorway nearby leads to the crypt, which has many intimate chapels set aside for private prayer and a display of cathedral and diocesan treasures. There is also much interesting graffiti and two pillars brought here from Reculver Towers (see page 50). Off the south-west transept is St Michael's Chapel, filled with monuments, including one to Sir George Rooke, a naval hero of the seventeenth century.

Near the east end of the cathedral are two very interesting monuments. One is to the Black Prince, who died in 1376. His body lay in state in Westminster Abbey for three months before being brought to Canterbury for burial. Above his tomb hang copies of his funeral achievements, whilst the originals are preserved nearby. On the opposite side of the cathedral is the tomb of Henry IV and his wife Joan of Navarre. It is a very elaborate tomb made of alabaster. Yet Becket, the most famous person associated with the cathedral, has no monument. His shrine was destroyed at the Reformation, although the elaborate pavement on which it stood survives, with superb tiles showing the signs of the Zodiac.

Stained glass is a major feature of Canterbury: the cathedral contains some of the best twelfth- and thirteenth-century work in England. Some of the windows have been reset at eye level, although it is still advisable to take binoculars to appreciate the detail. When originally completed, the windows told a series of stories, but, having been reset, they no longer follow a pattern and it is not easy to identify the scenes.

There are regular guided tours of the building and visitors may find them useful to understand the details of this large and complicated building. There is an admission charge for entry to the Cathedral Precincts and therefore a substantial amount of time should be allowed in order to make the most of a visit.

Canterbury: St Augustine's Abbey. Telephone: 01227 767345.
Open daily.

The abbey ruins stand to the east of the city, a few minutes walk outside the walls. They date in part from AD 598, when Augustine founded a church here as the burial place for the early Christian kings of Kent and for the bishops, later archbishops, who were to succeed him. Following the Norman Conquest the church was entirely rebuilt, although the Saxon church of St Pancras, to the east of the abbey, survived. After the Reformation part of the abbey was converted into a royal palace but it was not much used and fell into complete disrepair by the end of the seventeenth century. The ruins are rather complicated and visitors are advised to take advantage of the excellent audio tour.

St Augustine founded this abbey at Canterbury in the sixth century.

Canterbury: St Martin.

This is the oldest parish church in England that is still in use. When Augustine arrived in Kent in AD 597 he discovered that King Ethelbert's wife, Queen Bertha, was already worshipping in this building. Much of the original building survives, with Roman bricks making up a large part of the walls, but it is not known whether they were put there by the Romans or were reused at a later date. It is certain, however, that Christian worship has been offered within these walls longer than in any other building in England and for that reason thousands of visitors come here each year. The twentieth-century writer Mary Tourtel, creator of Rupert Bear, is buried on a small terrace in the churchyard, to the north-east of the church.

Challock: St Cosmas and St Damian. (North of Ashford, south of A252.)

This isolated country church displays some exceptional twentieth-century murals. These were painted in the 1950s and 1960s following a complete restoration of the building, which had been badly damaged in the Second World War. The earlier set was painted by two art students, the more recent set by John Ward RA. They are an exceptional contrast, the earlier in cartoon form, the later in a naturalistic style with figures in contemporary costume much influenced by the work of the Bloomsbury Group at Berwick in Sussex. Another rare feature at Challock is the Prickett Beam, a medieval 'curtain rail' to veil the altar from view during Lent, topped by candles, or 'pricketts'.

Chilham: St Mary. (South-west of Canterbury, south of A252.)

This large sombre church stands at the opposite side of the village square to Chilham Castle. Much of the character of the church derives from the nineteenth-century stained glass which fills almost every window of the building. There are some exceptional memorials. One is to Sir Dudley Digges, who lived in the early seventeenth century. It is constructed of Bethersden marble, a local stone that can be polished to produce a high shine. Another shows nineteenth-century children

playing games.

Cobham: St Mary Magdalene. (South-east of Gravesend, south of A2.)

Although Cobham is a delightful village and the church is worthy of inclusion as an architectural study in itself, it is the memorial brasses that attract the visitor. Here is the largest collection of monumental brasses in the world, dating from 1320 to 1529. The material of which they are made, latten, was imported from the continent, and the earlier ones are larger, because latten became harder to obtain as time went on and so brasses had to be made smaller. Most are to the de Cobham family and their descendants the Brookes. Brass-rubbers are welcome by appointment (telephone: 01474 814262). Behind the church is the New College of Cobham (see page 75).

Cranbrook: St Dunstan.

A unique feature of this church is a font designed for baptism by full immersion in the early eighteenth century. It was an attempt to draw worshippers from the then expanding Baptist congregation. The parson, John Johnson, decided to offer the same facilities as the Baptists and built a coffin-like tank at the top of a flight of steps to the room over the porch. It was never a success and only one baptism in it is recorded. The large table at the back of the church is an eighteenth-century sounding board removed from the pulpit in the nineteenth century, whilst some good windows by Charles Eamer Kempe (died 1907) are identified by his logo of a single wheatsheaf.

Doddington: the Beheading of St John the Baptist. (South-east of Sittingbourne, south of M2.)

This charming church, hidden amongst country lanes, contains much of interest. The south chapel belonged to the owners of nearby Sharsted Court and displays a good selection of memorials from the thirteenth century to the present day. On the north side of the chancel is a fine low-side window which allowed a kneeling priest to ring a bell at mass, and there are some large medieval wall-paintings. A medieval screen to the south of the chancel has a fine canopied priest's seat and there is a good Royal Arms on display at the west end.

Dode: Our Lady of the Meadows. Telephone: 01622 734205. (Near Luddesdowne, south of Gravesend, west of A228. OS 178: TQ 668638.)

This privately owned Norman church is unique in presenting the appearance of a church that 'survived' the Reformation. The Black Death destroyed the village in 1348 and the church was abandoned shortly afterwards, falling into disrepair. It was restored by a local antiquary in the early twentieth century and is now maintained by a trust which allows interested groups to use the building for multi-faith worship. A visit is essential for those with more than a passing interest in churches.

Eastwell: St Mary. (North of Ashford, west of A251.)
Open access to the church ruins.

The church became ruined as a result of neglect during the Second World War, when the park in which it stands was requisitioned by the military and public access was denied. It is one of the few ruined parish churches in the county. Its location is charming, standing next to a medieval stone house on the banks of a 40 acre (16 hectare) lake. The church is now owned by a national charity, the Friends of Friendless Churches, and draws many visitors because it contains the grave of Richard Plantagenet, illegitimate son of Richard III, who fled here after his father's death at the battle of Bosworth in 1485. The church is difficult to find but is well worth the journey.

Fairfield: St Thomas à Becket. (North-east of Rye, north of A259.)

There is no more remarkable church in Kent. It stands completely isolated in the Romney Marshes with not even a tree for company. Until quite recently it was cut off by flood waters in winter and even today the only way to reach it is by walking across a grassy causeway. It is a tiny two-cell building of timber-framed construction infilled with brick. Inside it retains an eighteenth-century atmosphere with box pews painted black and white and rails around the altar on three sides. Although the church was taken down and rebuilt in 1913 this work is hard to detect and for atmosphere this charming building is second to none. Services are held regularly and visitors are most warmly welcomed.

The church of St Thomas à Becket at Fairfield stands in the Romney Marshes.

Faversham: St Mary of Charity.

The first thing one notices about the church is the spire, which is similar to the 'crowns' of Scotland and was built in 1797 to replace a smaller tower made unsafe by an explosion at the local gunpowder factory in 1780. Inside, the transepts are unusual in having aisles; this is one of only four parish churches in England to show this feature. The nave is eighteenth-century and contrasts well with the surviving medieval work. There are misericords and wall-paintings.

Goudhurst: St Mary. (East of Tunbridge Wells, on A262.)

It is said that from the tower fifty-one other churches may be seen. Even from the church-yard the views are spectacular. The tower dates from the seventeenth century although the church is three hundred years earlier. Its main interest lies in the memorials which range from a fifteenth-century memorial brass to the wooden effigies of Sir Alexander and Lady Culpeper, who died in 1537. Wooden effigies are uncommon and these retain some of their original colouring.

Hollingbourne: All Saints. (East of Maidstone, on B2163.)

On 21st May 1382 a great earthquake shook this part of Kent and the church at Hollingbourne was badly damaged. As a result the interior looks rather odd, with roofs that do not line up. To the north is the seventeenth-century Culpeper Chapel, dominated by the marble monument to Lady Elizabeth Culpeper, who died in 1638. The inscription describes her as 'the best of women, best of wives, best of mothers'. Also in the church is the famous Culpeper Needlework, probably a funeral pall, worked in the seventeenth century by four Culpeper ladies. It is purple in colour, with a border of fruits including local cobnuts and hops. Because of its fragility it is not on permanent display. Near the church is the red-brick manor house, one of the former homes of the Culpepers.

Hornes Place Chapel, Appledore. (South-east of Tenterden, north of B2080.) English Heritage.

Open on Wednesdays only in summer.

This interesting fourteenth-century chapel once served a manor house. Although many private houses had chapels of this type before the Reformation, few survive today. The nearby parish church of Appledore has a nineteenth-century stained glass window depicting Hornes Place chapel.

Ickham: St John the Evangelist. (East of Canterbury, north of A257.)

This is a remarkable church of thirteenth-century date, with a very marked difference between the floor levels of the nave and the chancel. There are transepts to north and south, each containing important memorials. To the north is the effigy of William de Heghtresbury, who died in 1372, whilst to the south may be found the tomb of Thomas de Baa, who died in 1339. To find two monuments of this early date in a Kent church is very unusual.

Kilndown: Christ Church. (South-east of Tunbridge Wells, north of A21.)

Kilndown church is very special. It is one of the earliest examples of true Gothic Revival in England and dates from the 1840s. It was one of the model churches of the Camden Society and inspired many other restorations and new churches. It gives a good impression of how a medieval church might have appeared if the materials and techniques of the Victorian age had been available to the builders. All the furnishings are brightly coloured, and particularly noticeable is the pulpit, copied from the thirteenth-century example at Beaulieu in Hampshire.

Mereworth: St Lawrence. (West of Maidstone, on A26.)

The sight of Mereworth church through the hop gardens is not easily forgotten. This church was built in 1736 to replace a medieval building destroyed by John Fane when the present Mereworth Castle was built. Its architect is not known. It is Palladian in style – a great rarity for Kent – with a portico, spire and aisled nave. Inside there are monuments rescued from the old church and some attractive *trompe-l'oeil* decoration. Above the altar

St Lawrence's church, Mereworth.

is a Diocletian window containing panels of heraldic glass which probably came from the old manor house. In the churchyard is the grave of the first recipient of the Victoria Cross.

Milton Chantry, Gravesend. English Heritage.
Open March to December, daily.
This chantry chapel dates from the fourteenth century and housed the tombs of the de Valence and Montechais families. It also served as a place of worship for a nearby leper hospital before the Reformation. Today it often houses exhibitions of local arts and crafts.

Minster Abbey, Minster in Sheppey. (South-east of Sheerness, on B2008.)
Today this building should be called the 'Abbey Church of St Mary and St Sexburga', for it is a parish church built around the remains of an abbey founded by Sexburga, queen of Kent, in the seventh century. The south doorway is a fine example of the transition from Norman to Early English architecture. Much Saxon walling remains in the north chapel and there are some excellent monuments. Adjacent to the tidy churchyard is the gatehouse, which is the only part of the monastic buildings to survive and now houses a local history museum (see page 91).

Minster Abbey, Minster in Thanet. Telephone: 01843 821254. (West of Ramsgate, south of A253.)
Open for one guided tour each day.
The abbey was founded by Domneva in about AD 670. Her daughter, St Mildred, became one of Kent's best-known saints. The abbey fell into disrepair after Danish raids and never fully recovered. Its lands were given to St Augustine's Abbey in Canterbury in the eleventh century and a small religious presence was maintained. At the Reformation the buildings became a farmhouse. In 1937 they were purchased by an order of Roman Catholic nuns, who have restored them to monastic use and built a new chapel. The nuns are highly skilled in their various fields and show visitors parts of the medieval buildings at set times.

Newenden: St Peter. (South-west of Tenterden, on A28.)
An eyecatching tower and spire of 1859 by G. M. Hills announce this tiny fragment of a medieval church, much reduced in size during the seventeenth century. It stands by the county boundary and is a familiar landmark to travellers coming from Sussex. The chancel dates from the 1930s and shows how sensitive some additions of that period can be. The font is a wonderful piece of the Norman period, with carvings of various beasts.

Patrixbourne: St Mary. (South-east of Canterbury, east of A2.)
This charming village church has a greater number of interesting furnishings than most.

The south door shows Norman carving at its best, with eight mass dials scratched into it! The church contains a large selection of seventeenth-century Swiss stained glass panels, including scenes of the Raising of Lazarus and St Elizabeth of Hungary. The Conyngham family are well represented by monuments throughout the church.

Rochester: Cathedral Church of Christ and the Blessed Virgin Mary. Telephone: 01634 843366.
Open daily.

The cathedral was founded in AD 604, although the present building dates only from the Norman period. The outline of the Saxon foundations can be picked out in the floor at the west end of the present building. The nave is constructed of piers of differing designs, almost as impressive as the better-known examples at Durham and Norwich. The junction of nave and crossing is rather odd. In 1201 a baker from Perth, William, was murdered when travelling through Rochester and buried in the cathedral. Very shortly afterwards miracles started to occur and his tomb became a shrine. The wealthy left offerings and these were used to rebuild the cathedral, starting at the east end, but the money ran out when the reconstruction had got as far as the crossing, leaving an ugly join between new and old stonework. It is the thirteenth-century work that gives Rochester its character, enriched with Purbeck marble shafting. Dickens thought the cathedral had an 'earthy' smell, and certainly the crypt, the second largest in England, has an atmosphere of its own. In the north transept is the tomb of Walter de Merton, founder of Merton College at Oxford. Incorporated into it is a twentieth-century stained glass window by Sir Ninian Comper; look for his logo, a wild strawberry flower. There are also memorials to Charles Dickens (see page 106) and Richard Watts.

St Nicholas at Wade: St Nicholas. (Southwest of Margate, north of A28.)

The tall fourteenth-century flint tower dominates the flat farmlands that stretch towards the sea. The porch has a parvise (room) above. Originally used to house valuables, it was used as a plumber's workshop in the eighteenth century. The Bridges Chapel, north of the chancel, contains some splendid marble monuments. Above the font can be seen traces of medieval stone vaulting – unusual for a village church.

Sandwich: St Peter.

The three medieval churches of Sandwich are all worth looking at, but St Peter's is of the greatest architectural interest. Its rare cupola finishes off the tower in a strangely continental fashion. In the seventeenth century the tower collapsed into the south aisle. The ruins were given to the town's Dutch community, who repaired it and used it as their place of worship. It is now cared for by the Churches Conservation Trust. Most of the furnishings have been removed, allowing the visitor to study the proportions and architecture of the building. There are some good memorials

The steps to the room above the porch of St Nicholas at Wade church.

and a fine crown-post roof.

Speldhurst: St Mary the Virgin. (North-west of Tunbridge Wells, west of A26.)

The student of nineteenth-century stained glass will need no introduction to Speldhurst. It is the textbook example of the work of Sir Edward Burne-Jones, the great Pre-Raphaelite artist. Most of the windows were designed by him and made by the firm of Morris & Company. The church dates from 1870 but stands on the site of at least three predecessors. In the churchyard is a memorial made of Coade stone, and opposite it is one of the oldest inns in Kent.

Trottiscliffe: St Peter and St Paul. (North-west of West Malling, north of A20.)

This is in one of the prettiest settings for a church in Kent, away from the village centre in the lee of the Downs. It is a simple rectangular building with some superb furnishings, including a pulpit that came from Westminster Abbey, with a sounding board supported on a palm tree. The altar rails have a unique 'churching box', where kneeling women placed thank offerings for the safe arrival of their babies. There is some excellent modern stained glass to commemorate Bishop Gundulf, who lived in the adjoining manor in the eleventh century. The artist Graham Sutherland is buried in the churchyard.

Waldershare: All Saints. (North of Dover, west of A256.)

Open by prior arrangement with the Earl of Guilford.

The church is privately owned and stands in the grounds of Waldershare Park. The nave is nineteenth-century, but the chancel is medieval and the north and south chapels date from the seventeenth and eighteenth cen-

turies. The south chapel was built to take the tomb of Susan Bertie and her husband, a very plain but impressive tomb chest with effigies. The north chapel, built in 1712, houses the enormous monument to Sir Henry Furness, who built the present mansion. The monument is tiered like a wedding cake and it is very difficult to see the top from the ground! There are four broken-hearted ladies at each corner, but with the passage of time many of them have gained broken limbs as well.

West Peckham: St Dunstan. (North-east of Tonbridge, west of B2016.)

This delightful country church shows work from the Saxon period onwards. This earliest period is represented by a double-splayed window in the tower. Under the tower is a Norman font. At the north-east corner is a most unusual family pew, built on a platform which created a burial vault beneath. It is panelled and furnished with table and chairs and has a separate gallery for the servants. Partly obscured by the pew is an earlier monument, whilst above hang several hatchments dating from the eighteenth and nineteenth centuries.

Wingham: St Mary. (East of Canterbury, on A257.)

A very large church built on a corner of the main street, St Mary's supported a college of priests during the middle ages. After the Reformation the church fell on hard times and the north aisle was demolished. A fund was started to rebuild it, but the collector ran off with the money and a further collection produced insufficient funds. Wooden pillars were used in the nave instead of stone. The south chapel contains monuments to the Oxenden family, one of which is a free-standing piece which incorporates ox heads at each corner as a play on their name.

7
Historic houses and gardens

Bedgebury National Pinetum, near Goudhurst, Cranbrook TN17 2SL (OS 188: TQ 715338). Telephone: 01580 211044.
Open daily.

Covering 300 acres (120 hectares), this is the most comprehensive collection of conifers in Europe, started as a joint venture between Kew Gardens and the Forestry Commission in 1921. The landscaped valley with stream and lake is delightful for walks and there is a visitor centre. The different species of conifers produce cones at different times of the year but the pinetum has more to offer than just conifers: there are azaleas in the spring and fungi in the autumn.

Belmont, Belmont Park, Throwley, Faversham ME13 0HH. Telephone: 01795 890202.
Open Easter to September, Saturdays, Sundays and bank holiday Mondays.

The Harris family has lived at Belmont since 1801. The house, built of brick but covered with mathematical tiles, dates from the late eighteenth century. Panels made of Coade stone are set into the space between the ground-floor windows and those of the first floor. The mansion contains the finest collection of clocks to be found in an English country house, collected by the fifth Lord Harris, whilst the other rooms shown display good-quality furniture and paintings, many with an Indian theme – successive Lords have been associated with India. The elevated grounds contain a pinetum and grotto, whilst a prospect tower has been converted into holiday accommodation by the Landmark Trust.

Boughton Monchelsea Place, Boughton Monchelsea, Maidstone ME17 4BU. Telephone: 01622 743120.

Open Easter to October, Sundays and bank holiday Mondays; also Wednesdays in summer.

The present house, built of local ragstone, dates from 1567 and was built by Robert Rudston, whose father had been Lord Mayor of London. He was involved with Sir Thomas Wyatt in the revolt against Queen Mary I (see also Cooling Castle, page 53) and Boughton Monchelsea Place was confiscated by the Crown. The following year he was allowed to buy it back, but at one and a half times the original price. As a result he could not afford to make any alterations to keep it up to date. Indeed, apart from a fine staircase of about 1680 and a few rooms that were gothicised in the later eighteenth century, the house remains little altered today. It has a fine collection of furniture and paintings. The present owner has brought many objects out of store to furnish new display rooms. The deer park and gardens are extensive and from the terrace there are superb views over the Weald of Kent. The whole house has a lived-in atmosphere.

Chartwell, near Westerham TN16 1PS. Telephone: 01732 866368. National Trust.
Open: April to October, Wednesday to Sunday and bank holiday Mondays; March and November, Saturdays, Sundays and Wednesdays.

The house stands on a steep wooded site and takes its name from a well or spring that was first mentioned in the fourteenth century. The present house is more or less a rebuilding of an older one bought by Sir Winston Churchill in 1922. It remained his home for the next forty years. Although the house cannot be described as pretty it does retain a tremendous atmosphere, especially noticeable

Boughton Monchelsea Place has fine views of its deer park and the Weald of Kent from the terrace.

in Churchill's study and the elegant dining room. There are plenty of display rooms and an exhibition which includes sound footage. The house becomes very busy in the summer and entrance is by timed ticket. The gardens are a delight, with pools and lakes constructed by Churchill, and a long expanse of brick wall that reminds us of his skill as a bricklayer.

Chiddingstone Castle, Chiddingstone, near Edenbridge TN8 7AD. Telephone: 01732 870347.
Open: June to September, Wednesday to Sunday; April, May and October, Sundays only.
Chiddingstone Castle is a Gothic Revival house standing in a landscaped park near the village of the same name. In part it is Tudor, but most of what is seen is later. The castellated exterior recalls the late eighteenth-century taste for romantic architecture. Yet the interest lies not in the building itself, which is a popular venue for civil weddings, but in its collections built up by Denys Eyre Bower, who died in 1977. He was an eccentric who bought items connected with the Royal House of Stuart, ancient Egypt and Japan. These rank today as the most important private col-

lections of their type apart from those of the Royal Family. The house is untouched by commercialism and the grounds have an air of peacefulness.

Cobham Hall, Cobham, Gravesend DA12 3BL. Telephone: 01474 824319 or 823371.
Open in April, July and August on Wednesdays, Thursdays and Sundays.
One of the stateliest homes in Kent, Cobham Hall is an international boarding school for girls. It is now open regularly during school holidays and is licensed for civil weddings. The house dates from the Tudor, Stuart and Georgian periods and is noted for its marble fireplaces and plasterwork. Whilst it is of necessity institutionalised it offers a great deal to those interested in architecture, the highlight of a visit being the great Gilt Hall. This room displays in the ceiling the arms of the Dukes of Lennox, the seventeenth-century owners of Cobham. There is much work by James Wyatt, who worked principally for the fourth Earl of Darnley at the end of the eighteenth century. It was he who designed the derelict mausoleum in the park; tradition says that it was never used

because the bishop refused to consecrate it! The park is being restored by a charitable trust and is best seen in the spring when the daffodils form seas of yellow on which the Hall appears to float.

Doddington Place Gardens, Doddington, Sittingbourne ME9 0BB. Telephone: 01795 886101.
Open May to September, Sundays, Wednesdays and bank holiday Mondays.

Most of the 10 acres (4 hectares) of gardens were laid out in the early twentieth century, except for the Wellingtonia avenue, which dates from the construction of the house in the 1860s. There are lovely views over the valley and surrounding countryside from the wide, yew-bordered lawns. There is a large Edwardian rock garden and a formal sunken garden which is particularly delightful in late summer.

Down House, Luxted Road, Downe, Orpington BR6 7JT. See the Darwin Museum, Downe, page 85.

Emmetts Garden, Ide Hill, Sevenoaks TN14 6AY. Telephone: 01732 750367. National Trust.
Open April to October, Saturdays, Sundays, Wednesdays and bank holiday Mondays, plus limited end of season openings.

This enjoyable garden was designed to make the most of a steeply sloping site, with many specimen trees and fine views. There are excellent spring and autumn displays and a pretty rock garden. Its proximity to Westerham makes it an ideal place to combine with a visit to that area.

Finchcocks, Goudhurst TN17 1HH. Telephone: 01580 211702.
Open Easter to September, Sundays and bank holidays; also Wednesdays and Thursdays in August.

The house dates from 1725 and is built of brick. Like Chiddingstone Castle it is more famous for its collections than its architecture for here is a unique set of period keyboard instruments. Guided tours and demonstrations are given. Hearing music appropriate to the period of the instrument being played makes a visit an authentic and enchanting experience.

Gad's Hill, Higham by Rochester ME3 7PA. Telephone: 01474 822366.
Open April to October on the first Sunday afternoon in each month and on bank holiday Sunday afternoons; also during the Rochester Dickens Festival and at other times by appointment.

This eighteenth-century house standing on the old road from London to Rochester is now used as a school. It was noticed by the young Charles Dickens, who told his father that one day he would like to own it. His father said that if he applied himself he would one day be able to afford it – and so he did! Dickens lived here from 1857 until his death in the house in 1870. His Swiss chalet (see page 91) stood in the shrubbery garden across the road, linked to the main garden by a tunnel under the road. Visitors see the rooms associated with Dickens, including his study, made famous by the engraving 'The Empty Chair' (see page 79).

Godinton House, Godinton Park, Ashford TN23 3BW. Telephone: 01233 612669.
Gardens open: Easter weekend; June to September, Sundays and bank holidays. House closed for renovation in 1997.

This medieval and later house is one of the most rewarding in Kent. Its homely feel – despite its large size – and furnishings of the highest quality make it surprising that it is not better known. Perhaps that is part of its charm. There are extensive collections of china and exquisite furniture and *objets d'art*. The large seventeenth-century staircase and carved panelling showing military volunteers have no equal in England. The gardens, which are at their finest in spring, date in the main from the nineteenth and twentieth centuries and it is difficult to realise that they are only 2 miles (3 km) from Ashford International station.

Goodnestone Park Gardens, near Wingham, Canterbury CT3 1PL. Telephone: 01304 840107.
Open April to October, daily except Tuesdays and Saturdays.

Frances Hodgson Burnett was inspired by the gardens at Great Maytham Hall to write 'The Secret Garden'.

There are many fine old trees in this 14 acre (5.7 hectare) garden set in unspoiled countryside. The extensive walled gardens with their magnificent borders make use of the village church as a focal point and the newly established woodland walk has been planned by Lady FitzWalter to make the most of the sylvan glades. Jane Austen's brother married a daughter of the house and Jane was a frequent visitor, using the house as inspiration for some of her work. This is one of the finest gardens in the county – certainly in one of the quietest settings. The house dates from the eighteenth century and is open only to groups by prior appointment.

Great Comp Garden, Comp Lane, Platt, Borough Green TN15 8QS. Telephone: 01732 882669.
Open April to October, daily.
    It is difficult to imagine that this 7 acre (3 hectare) garden dates only from the late 1950s. It was planned and planted by Mr and Mrs Roderick Cameron with heathers, terraces and woodland walks. There are different vistas and atmospheres at each turn of the paths, making this an interesting garden to explore from spring to autumn.

Great Maytham Hall, Rolvenden TN17 4NE. Telephone: 01580 241346.
Open May to September, Wednesday and Thursday afternoons.
    Great Maytham was designed by Sir Edwin Lutyens in 1910 and ranks as one of his most successful houses in Kent. It now belongs to the Country Houses Association and only the principal rooms are shown. The gardens are of special interest because they provided the inspiration for Frances Hodgson Burnett's *The Secret Garden* when she lived in the house.

Groombridge Place Gardens and Enchanted Forest, Groombridge, Tunbridge Wells TN3 9QG. Telephone: 01892 863999.
Open April to October, daily.
    Groombridge Place is best-known as the setting for the film *The Draughtsman's Contract* and its 164 acres (66 hectares) of parkland and gardens, set in a valley, provide a magical day out. There are good water gardens, and newly established walks through the 'Enchanted Forest' contrast well with the tightly formal gardens near the house. Boat rides are available and flying displays by birds of prey are given.

Hall Place, Bourne Road, Bexley DA5 1PQ. Telephone: 01322 526574.
Open: telephone for details.
    This unusual house, part Tudor, part Jacobean, contains displays relating to local history as well as changing art exhibitions. The extensive gardens have been restored to provide many differing habitats, and walks along the river take visitors to the more open playing fields that have been created from former parkland.

Ightham Mote, Ivy Hatch, Ightham, Sevenoaks TN15 0NT. Telephone: 01732 810378. National Trust.
Open April to October, daily except Tuesdays and Saturdays.
    Ightham Mote stands in a remote valley

Ightham Mote is one of the most attractive medieval moated buildings in England.

and forms one of the most attractive groups of medieval moated buildings in England. The present house is a mixture of periods, but the predominant style is fourteenth-century. The great hall is one of the most notable rooms and should be compared with the great halls at nearby Knole and Penshurst. During its early history the house had owners of mainly local importance, but during the late sixteenth and seventeenth centuries it was the home of the Selby family, important courtiers. Dame Dorothy Selby, lady-in-waiting to Elizabeth I, was an excellent needlewoman, as her monument in Ightham church shows. One of her descendants, Sir Charles Selby, was fined £500 in 1663 for running naked down Fleet Street! There is much of interest for the visitor.

Knole, Sevenoaks TN15 0RP. Telephone: 01732 450608. National Trust.
Open April to October, Wednesday to Sunday (afternoons only on Thursdays).
    Knole is one of the largest private houses in Britain. Building started in 1457 for Thomas Bourchier, Archbishop of Canterbury, although there had probably been an earlier

house here. In the sixteenth century Henry VIII took possession from Archbishop Cranmer, and it was he who extended the house almost to the extent that the visitor sees today. Elizabeth I gave it to Sir Thomas Sackville and it is still the home of the Sackville-West family. The setting is memorable. The house stands on a small hill in the middle of a vast deer park. Behind the house is a walled garden. Many of the rooms contain furniture made for them in the seventeenth century, including the famous Knole Settee. One upper room has a 'dumb bell', a type of bell rope with a weight on the end that was used for exercise! There are many portraits of the family and of monarchs and also three state beds. The lighting levels in the house are kept extremely low to protect furnishings. The gardens, which are maintained by Lord Sackville, are open only one day a week in the summer.

Lullingstone Castle, Eynsford, Dartford DA4 0JA. Telephone: 01322 862114.
Open April to September, Saturdays, Sundays and bank holidays, afternoons only.
    There   are   three   components   to

The Sackville-West family still lives at Knole, one of the largest private houses in Britain.

Lullingstone: the gatehouse, built of brick in 1497 and one of the earliest of its type in England; the parish church, full of eighteenth-century furnishings; and the house, Lullingstone Castle, essentially eighteenth-century on the outside but older within. The three face each other across a wide lawn, forming a most delightful setting. The castle is still a family home and the six rooms shown have a great deal of interest, much of it pertaining to the frequent visits of Queen Anne in the early eighteenth century. Much was done to make her comfortable, including the erection of a bath-house, now ruined, on the banks of the river at the back of the house.

The new staircase in the Castle was built with very shallow treads so that the portly queen could ascend them unaided! All is pleasantly uncommercialised.

Maison Dieu, Ospringe, Faversham ME13 8TS. Telephone: 01795 534542 or 533751.
Open April to October, Saturdays, Sundays and bank holidays.

The Maison Dieu was founded in the thirteenth century as a hospital and shelter for pilgrims on their way to the abbey at Faversham and the shrine of St Thomas at Canterbury. Its lower walls are constructed of flint rubble, whilst its jettied upper floor is timber-framed. There is a small museum of archaeological finds and displays relating to the history of the area. The nearby ruins of Stone church, abandoned in the sixteenth century, are also worth visiting, incorporating the walls of a pagan Roman shrine.

Marle Place Gardens, Marle Place Road, Brenchley, Tonbridge TN12 7HS. Telephone: 01892 722304.
Open April to October, daily.
A selection of different gardens includes woodland, walled and scented gardens and ponds. A rockery and herbaceous borders have been established around the seventeenth-century house. The gardens cover 10 acres (4 hectares) and there are many unusual feature plants and good autumn colour.

Mount Ephraim Gardens, Hernhill, Faversham ME13 9TX. Telephone: 01227 751496.
Open mid April to September, daily.
The present gardens were laid out in 1912. By the time of the Second World War they had become overgrown but have now been restored. Terraces of roses lead to a small lake

and a woodland area. There is an excellent collection of trees and shrubs, including rhododendrons and topiary, a large Japanese rock garden and a vineyard. There are exceptional views across the Thames estuary.

The New College of Cobham, Cobham, near Gravesend DA12 3BX. Telephone: 01474 814280.
Open daily except Thursdays (also closed Fridays in winter).
These delightful almshouses nestle behind the parish church (see page 63). Originally a chantry college for priests attached to the church, they now house retired people. One of the two original courtyards has gone but the surviving one is beautifully maintained and the Great Hall, which is open to visitors, has a fine atmosphere.

Northbourne Court Gardens, Northbourne, near Deal CT14 0LW. Telephone: 01304 611281.
Open June, July and August, Sunday afternoons only.
This Tudor terraced garden is built on the site of the palace of the Saxon kings of Kent.

Owletts, in the village of Cobham, is an attractive seventeenth-century house.

A series of walled enclosures provides sheltered habitats for chalk-loving plants.

Old Soar Manor, Plaxtol, Borough Green TN15 0QX. Telephone: 01892 890651.
Open April to September, daily.

Old Soar is a fine example of part of a thirteenth-century country manor house built with a solar and chapel over an undercroft by the Culpepper family of Aylesford. It is reached by a very narrow lane, more reminiscent of Devon than Kent. There is a small display on the history of the property. The attached farmhouse, built on the site of the medieval great hall, is not open to the public, but the surviving solar with ensuite lavatory and chapel is one of the finest medieval domestic structures to survive in the county.

Owletts, Cobham, near Gravesend DA12 3AP. Telephone: 01892 890651. National Trust.
Open April to September, Wednesdays and Thursdays.

Owletts is a red brick house built at the end of the seventeenth century. It has some fine ceilings, a contemporary staircase and a clock which shows the time in all parts of the Commonwealth. Owletts stands at a junction formerly called Rookery Corner, although the tall avenue that was once home to the rooks has given way to a snowdrop meadow.

Owl House Gardens, Lamberhurst, Tunbridge Wells. Telephone: 01892 890963.
Open daily.

This old English garden, created by the Marchioness of Dufferin and Ava around a timber-framed smuggler's cottage, is delightful at all times of the year, but especially in spring when daffodils line the woodland walks. There are water gardens, rare shrubs and mature trees. Admission fees go Lady Dufferin's charity for arthritics.

Penshurst Place, Penshurst, Tonbridge TN11 8DG. Telephone: 01892 870307.
Open: April to September, daily; March and October, weekends only.

The internationally renowned great hall, built in the fourteenth century, forms the core of this large house. In the sixteenth century Edward VI granted it to his steward, Sir William Sidney. Sir Philip Sidney was a favourite of Elizabeth I and is famous as a soldier and poet. The house is still the home of the Sidney family and the show rooms contain good family portraits, tapestries and furniture. The gardens are a delight and include formal borders, orchards and pools. There is a children's playground, nature trail and toy museum.

The Pines Gardens, Beach Road, St Margaret's Bay. Telephone: 01304 852764.
Open daily.

These delightful gardens, with spectacular views of the famous white cliffs, cover 6 acres (2.4 hectares) and are renowned for their trees, plants, lake and waterfall. There is a statue of Sir Winston Churchill, a wishing well and picnic area. There are numerous seats and facilities for the elderly and disabled.

Quebec House, Westerham TN16 1TD. Telephone: 01959 562206. National Trust.
Open April to October, Tuesdays only.

The gabled red brick house dates mainly from the seventeenth century and was the boyhood home of General James Wolfe, whose statue stands on the village green. The four rooms on view contain portraits, prints and memorabilia relating to the great soldier and his family, and in the former coach-house there is an exhibition about his famous victory over the French at Quebec in 1759.

Quex House, Quex Park, Birchington CT7 0BH. Telephone: 01843 842168.
Open: telephone for details.

This unusual Regency mansion stands in historic gardens surrounded by a large park a short distance from the coast. Several furnished rooms in the house are open to the public adjacent to the nine-gallery Powell-Cotton Museum of African and Asian exhibits. The museum is of international importance and was established at the end of the nineteenth century by Major Powell-Cotton, a distinguished naturalist, anthropologist, photographer, collector and big-game hunter.

The park, which is not open to the public, is distinguished by two towers (not accessible), constructed by John Powell Powell in the early nineteenth century, one of which houses a unique peal of twelve bells, which are rung regularly.

Riverhill House Gardens, Riverhill, Sevenoaks TN15 0RR. Telephone: 01732 458802 or 452557.
Open April, May and June, Sundays and bank holiday weekends.
The gardens of this lived-in family house command superb views over the Weald. The historic hillside garden features rhododendrons, azaleas and bluebells in a woodland setting.

St Johns Jerusalem, Sutton at Hone, Dartford DA4 9HQ. Telephone: 01892 890651. National Trust.
Open April to October, Wednesdays only.
Built as a commandery of the Knights Hospitallers in the middle ages, St Johns Jerusalem was later converted into a private house. In the eighteenth century it was the home of Edward Hasted, the Kent historian. Only the chapel and the gardens leading down to the river are open to the public.

Sissinghurst Castle Garden, Sissinghurst, near Cranbrook TN17 2AB. Telephone: 01580 715330. National Trust.
Open April to October, daily except Mondays.
Sissinghurst is known for its delightful gardens laid out by Vita Sackville-West and Harold Nicolson in the 1930s. Yet here too are the remains of an Elizabethan house built by Sir Richard Baker in 1570. Elizabeth I stayed here on her progress through the county three years later, but the expense of entertaining his monarch put too much strain on Sir Richard, who was forced to abandon the castle shortly afterwards. In the eighteenth century it was used to house French prisoners of war. After that most of the buildings were demolished, leaving just the gatehouse tower and stables. These were restored by the Nicolsons to form a backdrop to their gardens, to which access is controlled by timed tickets to avoid overcrowding.

Smallhythe Place, Small Hythe, Tenterden TN30 7NG. Telephone: 01580 762334. National Trust.

St Johns Jerusalem viewed from the gardens, which are open regularly during the summer.

Open April to October, Saturday to Wednesday.

Smallhythe Place was built for a Kentish yeoman in the sixteenth century. The valley below was originally a shipbuilder's yard until the river Rother changed its course and its tributary silted up completely at the end of the nineteenth century. From 1889 until 1928 the house was the home of the actress Dame Ellen Terry and today it contains a fascinating collection of theatrical memorabilia. The atmosphere of the house is almost as if Dame Ellen left it yesterday. The Barn Theatre nearby is usually open at the same time as the house, but the house does suffer from overcrowding and only twenty-five people are allowed inside at one time.

Squerryes Court, Westerham TN16 1SJ. Telephone: 01959 562345 or 563118.
Open April to September, Wednesdays, Saturdays, Sundays and bank holiday Mondays.

Squerryes was built in 1681 by Sir Nicholas Crisp. The Warde family purchased the house in the early eighteenth century and still live there. The house is typical of its date, being built of warm red brick with beautifully proportioned rooms. There are good eighteenth-century furnishings including tapestries and paintings, and also some memorabilia of General Wolfe. Wolfe received his first commission whilst standing in the gardens and a memorial was later erected to commemorate this event. The grounds include an extensive lake, an eighteenth-century dovecote and a fine formal garden.

Stoneacre, Otham, Maidstone ME15 8RS. Telephone: 01622 862871. National Trust.
Open April to October, Wednesdays and Saturdays.

Stoneacre is typical of the many timber-framed houses in Kent. It dates from the fifteenth century and was built as a hall-house

with a central hall that rose the full height of the building. As new ideas and practices came into being it was altered and it remains a comfortable family house. In 1920 it was bought by a keen antiquarian, Aymer Vallance, who set about restoring it. He brought in furnishings and architectural details from other old houses to form a structure very much in keeping with the fifteenth-century original.

Temple Manor, Strood, Rochester. Telephone: 01634 827980. Rochester upon Medway City Council.
Open by prior arrangement only.

Temple Manor was a house of the Knights Templar, an order of celibate soldiers whose task was to protect pilgrims travelling to the Holy Land. It was probably used by one of their officials, providing a convenient stopping place between Dover and London. It has a thirteenth-century undercroft, on which stands a great stone chamber. During the seventeenth century a brick wing was added to make it into a comfortable farmhouse. In the 1930s it was rescued from complete ruin by Rochester City Council. Despite being surrounded by a railway, warehouses and factories, it is a delightful and unexpected building.

Yalding Organic Gardens, Benover Road, Yalding ME18 6EX. Telephone: 01622 814650.
Open: May to September, Wednesday to Sunday; April and October, weekends only.

These gardens provide a magnificent tour through gardening history, from a medieval herb garden, through a Tudor knot garden and a Victorian cottage garden to a 1950s allotment. There is an organic garden, a water garden and a wildflower area, set against a typical Kent backdrop of hop gardens and oast houses.

8
Museums

Ashford

Ashford Borough Museum, The Churchyard, Ashford TN23 1QG. Telephone: 01233 623845.
Open March to November, Monday to Saturday.

This interesting small museum details the history of the market and railway town of Ashford and the surrounding villages.

Beltring

Whitbread Hop Farm, Beltring, Paddock Wood TN12 6PY. Telephone: 01622 872068.
Open daily.

This agricultural museum is situated in the largest group of Victorian oast houses in the world. Displays chart the progress of the hops from bines to beer. Oast houses were mainly constructed during the eighteenth and nineteenth centuries to dry hops before packing them into special sacks called hop pockets. It is essential that the hops are bone-dry before packing. They were spread out on the upper floor of the oast kiln and a furnace was lit underneath. The white cowls at the top of the structure caused a draught to draw the warm air up inside. Today few oasts are in use and it is interesting to visit this museum to see how they work. A popular feature at the Whitbread Hop Farm is the Shire horses, now a permanent attraction.

Birchington

Powell-Cotton Museum, Quex House, Quex Park, Birchington CT7 0BH. See Quex House, page 76.

Brenzett

Brenzett Aeronautical Museum, Brenzett, Romney Marsh. Telephone: 01233 627911.
Open Easter to October, weekends and Wednesdays; also Thursdays and Fridays in summer.

This display of items connected with aeronautics is a good introduction to the subject and contains a wide range of relics from both British and German aircraft of the Second World War, together with aircraft armaments, maps and photographs.

Broadstairs

Bleak House Museum, Fort Road, Broadstairs CT10 1EY. Telephone: 01843 862224.
Open March to October, daily.

This house was for many years the holiday home of Charles Dickens, and some of the rooms on view are shown as they were in his time. Other rooms house displays of maritime artefacts and objects salvaged from local wrecks. There is a large smuggling display in the cellars. In the room which Dickens used as a study is the chair which is the very one depicted in the famous picture 'The Empty Chair', showing Dickens's desk at Gad's Hill the day after his death (see page 71). The house is not the building that features in his novel *Bleak House*. It was called Fort House in his day and was renamed thirty years after his death.

The Crampton Tower Museum, The Broadway, High Street, Broadstairs CT10 2AB. No telephone.
Open Easter to early October, Mondays, Tuesdays, Thursdays, Fridays and bank holiday Sundays, afternoons only.

This museum is housed in two buildings which were built as the town's first public waterworks. Crampton Tower itself, built in 1859 by Thomas Russell Crampton (1816-88), a notable civil engineer and native of Broadstairs, contains his drawings and patents and some railway items. The second building contains items related to transport, including the railways and tramways of Thanet, the Broadstairs to Canterbury stagecoach and two working layouts.

The Whitbread Hop Farm at Beltring stables the famous Whitbread Shire horses.

Dickens House Museum, 2 Victoria Parade, Broadstairs CT10 1QS (on the main seafront). Telephone: 01843 862853.
Open Easter to mid October, daily.

This is the house where Dickens found inspiration for the character of Miss Betsy Trotwood, David Copperfield's aunt. In the parlour, now furnished as he described it, Dickens and his son Charlie watched Miss Mary Strong chase the donkeys and donkey boys away from her house. Other rooms contain displays relating to Dickens and Broadstairs, and costume and Victoriana. Bequeathed to the town by Dora Tattam, the museum was opened in 1973. Few houses have such a lovely view across the bay – a scene little changed since Dickens knew it.

Canterbury

Canterbury Heritage, Poor Priests' Hospital, Stour Street, Canterbury. Telephone: 01227 452747.
Open Monday to Saturday; also open Sundays in peak season.

This exciting museum of the history of Canterbury is located within the beautifully restored Poor Priests' Hospital, away from the noisy High Street. Holograms, computer-generated displays, costumed figures and an audio-visual display make it one of the most up-to-date museums in the county. By careful selection from their large holdings, the curators have been able to show a comprehensive history of the city in an interesting fashion. Amongst the varied exhibits is one on the Whitstable to Canterbury Railway, the first passenger line in the world.

The Canterbury Tales, St Margaret's Street, Canterbury. Telephone: 01227 454888.
Open daily.

In the setting of a medieval church, audio-visual scenes from Chaucer's *Canterbury Tales* recreate the pilgrimage from London to the shrine of St Thomas à Becket. It provides an intriguing glimpse of life in the fourteenth century with authentic sounds and smells!

Royal Museum and Art Gallery, High Street, Canterbury CT1 2JE. Telephone:

The covered slips and Upper Mast House at Chatham Historic Dockyard.

Quex House, Birchington, was the home of Major Powell-Cotton, whose natural history and ethnographic collection is displayed in the adjacent museum.

01227 452747.
Open daily except Sundays.

Housed in the high-Victorian Beaney Institute, the displays include fine porcelain, glass, jewellery, Victorian toys and the archaeology of east Kent. There are also galleries devoted to The Buffs and the city's collection of landscape and animal paintings by Thomas Sidney Cooper, who lived nearby.

Westgate Museum, Westgate Tower, Canterbury. Telephone: 01227 452747.
Open daily except Sundays.

This museum of military history – arms, armour and guns – is housed in the only remaining medieval gateway into the city, next to the charming gardens alongside the river Stour.

Chatham

Chatham Historic Dockyard, Chatham ME4 4TE. Telephone: 01634 812551.
Open April to October, daily.

Since its closure the former naval dockyard has been undergoing restoration to show its four hundred years of history. A living and working museum has been created where some of the older crafts have been revived. Much has changed since Nelson's *Victory* was built here, but the Ropery, the covered slipways and listed buildings preserve the unique maritime atmosphere. An excellent display charts the history of wooden warships and one can visit HMS *Gannet*, built in 1878, the flag loft and the museum. A recent addition is the lifeboat collection of the Royal National Lifeboat Institution; it comprises fifteen craft, including a Blue Peter lifeboat, and displays about famous rescues.

Medway Heritage Centre, St Mary's Church, Dock Road, Chatham ME4 4SH. Telephone: 01634 407116.
Open daily.

The heritage centre provides an informative look at the history of the river Medway and the people who, throughout history, have relied on it for their livelihood. It is housed in the redundant church of St Mary, whose churchyard commands fine views over the river and dockyard.

Cranbrook

Cranbrook Museum, Carriers Road, Cranbrook TN17 3JX. Telephone: 01580 714349.
Open: April to September, Tuesday to Saturday; March, October and November, Wednesdays, Thursdays and Saturdays only.

This museum is housed in a delightful timber-framed house just off the main street and contains much of local interest. Formerly the rectory, it was made into four cottages before later being converted to house the museum. The town relied on the cloth industry for much of the middle ages and the relevant display includes a piece of local broadcloth. A large collection of stuffed birds and other local items, including displays on the famous Cranbrook Colony of artists, add considerably to the interest of one of the best small museums in Kent.

Dartford

Dartford Borough Museum, Market Street, Dartford DA1 1EU. Telephone: 01322 343555.
Open every afternoon except Wednesdays and Sundays.

This small museum illustrates the geology, archaeology and social history of the town and surrounding area. Interesting exhibits include a partial reconstruction of a draper's shop complete with working 'cash railway', local fossils and a wealth of archaeological objects spanning 250,000 years of human history. Pride of place goes to the Darenth Bowl discovered in 1978 in the grounds of a nearby hospital. This Saxon bowl, dating from the fifth century, is decorated with Christian symbols. This suggests the continuing influence of Christianity following the collapse of the Roman Empire.

Deal

Deal Maritime and Local History Museum, 22 St George's Road, Deal CT14 2AB. Telephone: 01304 372679.
Open end of May to end of September, daily.

This small but fascinating collection of charts, pictures and local memorabilia is housed just off the High Street. There is special reference to maritime and garrison history.

Time Ball Tower, Victoria Parade, Deal CT14 7BP. Telephone: 01304 201066.
Open July and August only, daily except Mondays.

This unique building was constructed as a semaphore station and later converted into a time-ball tower. The ball on top of the tower was raised and dropped each day at 1.00 pm to enable ships to set their clocks accurately. The tower has been restored and now houses a museum of time and telegraphy with working models and historical displays. The time ball is dropped for the benefit of visitors.

Victoriana Exhibition, Town Hall, Deal CT14 6BB. Telephone: 01304 210200.
Open July and August only, daily except Mondays.

This exhibition of everyday objects and works of art tells the story of the Victorians and the remarkable society in which they lived.

Dover

Dover Museum, Market Square, Dover CT16 1PB. Telephone: 01304 201066.
Open daily.

Opened in 1991, this purpose-built museum is devoted to the history of Dover since prehistoric times, with changing exhibitions.

Dover Transport Museum, Old Park Barracks, Whitfield, Dover CT16 2HQ. Telephone: 01304 204612.
Open Easter to October on Sundays; in summer additionally on Thursdays and Fridays.

In this newly housed museum cars, commercial vehicles, cycles and motorcycles are displayed in a setting accessible to the disabled.

Old Town Gaol, Biggin Street, Dover CT16 1DQ. Telephone: 01304 242766.
Open: in summer, daily; in winter, daily except Mondays and Tuesdays.

Beneath the town hall visitors can see fourteen cells with washrooms and an exercise yard brought to life to show the horrors of life behind bars in the nineteenth century – a fascinating experience!

The Princess of Wales's Royal Regiment and Queen's Regimental Museum, Dover Castle, Dover CT16 1HU. Telephone: 01304 240121.
Open daily.

The museum of the Queen's Regiment is displayed in part of Dover Castle and is open as part of the castle's usual attractions.

The White Cliffs Experience, Market Square, Dover CT16 1PB. Telephone: 01304 210101.
Open daily.

This award-winning new hands-on experience in the centre of Dover brings to life Britain during the Roman occupation. Attractions also include a 1940s Dover street, an end of pier show and, for children, Gromet's Challenge.

Down House, Downe, was the home of Charles Darwin for forty years and now houses the Darwin Museum.

Maison Dieu, Ospringe, was built to shelter pilgrims on their way to Faversham and Canterbury.

Fordwich's town hall is reputedly the smallest in England and now houses a local museum.

Downe

The Darwin Museum, Down House, Luxted Road, Downe BR6 7JT. Telephone: 01689 859119. English Heritage.

Reopening in summer 1997 after renovation; telephone for opening details.

This interesting house was the home of Charles Darwin for forty years. There are collections of Darwin's writings and possessions and one may walk along the woodland path where he did much of his thinking.

Dymchurch

The Law of the Levels, New Hall, New Hall Close, Dymchurch TN29 0LF. Telephone: 01303 872142.

Open on Tuesday, Wednesday and Thursday afternoon.

This museum of the history of Romney Marsh and its management over the centuries is housed in the former sixteenth-century courtroom. Although it is a small display, the setting is unique and it should not be missed.

Faversham

Fleur de Lis Heritage Centre, 13 Preston Street, Faversham ME13 8NS. Telephone: 01795 534542.

Open daily except Sundays (but open Sundays in summer).

This award-winning museum and heritage centre is housed in the former Fleur de Lis inn. The visitor can enjoy a short audiovisual display before exploring the many collections and montages arranged by the Faversham Society. The society was formed in 1962, since when it has flourished. In 1977 it opened the Heritage Centre, which is used as a model by similar societies across Britain. It is also responsible for the Chart Gunpowder Mill (see page 97) and Maison Dieu, Ospringe (page 74). Displays relate primarily to the town and an interesting transport display includes a 1905 speed restriction sign allowing vehicles to travel at no more than 8 mph (13km/h). In the low-vaulted cellars are larger exhibits whilst the ground floor contains a tourist information office and an excellent Kentish Bookshop.

Folkestone

Folkestone Museum and Art Gallery, Grace Hill, Folkestone CT20 1HD. Telephone: 01303 850123.

Open daily except Sundays.

This general museum has displays of local and natural history, archaeology and applied art. The gallery has changing exhibitions of both local and national appeal.

Fordwich

Fordwich Town Hall, King Street, Fordwich, Canterbury. Telephone: 01227 710358.

Open: telephone for details.

This charming timber-framed building is reputed to be the smallest town hall in England. It was built about 1540 when Fordwich was an important port on the banks of the river Stour. Now the place is a small village away from the hustle and bustle of Canterbury. The town hall contains much of local historical interest, including the famous ducking stool. The crane which unloaded goods for Canterbury may be seen beside the river.

The Fleur de Lis Heritage Centre in Faversham.

The Royal Engineers Museum in Gillingham has been enlarged to include exciting reconstructions of the Engineers' present-day work overseas.

Gillingham

Royal Engineers Museum, Prince Arthur Road, Gillingham ME4 4UG. Telephone: 01634 406397.
Open daily (on Fridays by appointment only).

This remarkable museum tells the story of Britain's soldier engineers from 1066 to the present day. The Royal Engineers introduced military flying, diving, wireless survey and photography, all included in the displays. The magnificent medal displays include twenty-four Victoria Crosses, three George Crosses, unique gallantry awards from the Falklands War and the regalia of Field Marshal Lord Kitchener. New post-1945 galleries include a 15 ton bulldozer dropped by parachute in the jungles of Borneo and a Harrier GR3 jump-jet in its hide.

Gravesend

Chantry Heritage Centre, Fort Gardens. Gravesend DA12 2BH. Telephone: 01474 321520.

Open daily.

This heritage centre charts the history of Gravesham from Roman times. Located in a Grade I listed building near the river front, it provides an ideal visit. Special events and exhibitions are staged.

Hawkinge

Kent Battle of Britain Museum, Aerodrome Road, Hawkinge, near Folkestone CT18 7AG. Telephone: 01303 893140.
Open Easter to end of October, daily.

This is the most important collection of Battle of Britain artefacts on show in Britain. The Dowding Memorial Hangar houses full-size replica aircraft used in the film *The Battle of Britain* (1968) and engines and other relics of German aircraft. The Stuart-Buttle Hangar contains full-size replicas of Hurricane and Spitfire fighters and vehicles used on a 1940s airfield. The Armoury contains a comprehensive collection of ground-based and airborne weaponry and a collection of uniforms, flying kit and insignia, British and German, worn in the Battle of Britain. The former Operations Block houses a collection of small items from some four hundred aircraft either donated to the museum or excavated by its recovery team, and in another building a V1 flying bomb can be seen.

Headcorn

Lashenden Air Warfare Museum, Headcorn Aerodrome, Headcorn, Ashford TN27 9HX. Telephone: 01622 890226.
Open Easter to October, Sundays and bank holiday Mondays only. (Parties at other times by appointment.)

This very interesting museum of aviation exhibits from 1911 to the present day has six aircraft including a piloted V1 flying bomb.

Herne Bay

Herne Bay Museum, 12 William Street, Herne Bay CT6 5EJ. Telephone: 01227 367368.
Open from summer 1997, daily.

This is a brand-new museum of Herne Bay shown in a series of displays, with an excellent collection of maps and old photographs located over two floors. There are sections on the development of the town, with a special feature on the pier which made the town famous and the nearby Reculver Towers (see page 50). A changing exhibition is held in the art gallery.

Hythe

Hythe Local History Room, Town Council Offices, Stade Street, Hythe CT21 6BG. Telephone: 01303 266152.
Open daily, except Sundays and bank holidays.

This small museum shows the history of the town and its role as a member of the Confederation of the Cinque Ports. Weights and measures and military history form part of the interesting displays.

Lydd

Lydd Town Museum, Old Fire Station, Lydd. Telephone: 01797 366566.
Open: Easter to mid July, weekends; mid July to end of October, daily.

A display of local artefacts includes an 1890s fire-engine and a station bus.

Maidstone

Maidstone Museum and Art Gallery, St Faith's Street, Maidstone ME14 1LH. Telephone: 01622 754497.
Open daily.

One of the finest traditional museums in south-east England, Maidstone Museum is housed in the Tudor Chillington Manor

The Great Hall at Maidstone Museum and Art Gallery.

These topiary chessmen are in the gardens of Hever Castle.

The white garden at Sissinghurst viewed from the top of the tower.

Goodnestone Park has associations with Jane Austen. Its gardens are open to visitors.

House. The outstanding collections include furniture, natural history and ceramics. Of particular interest are the displays on local industry, one of the earliest stained glass windows designed by Sir Edward Burne-Jones, and a wonderful Japanese gallery. The museum also houses the Royal West Kent Regiment Gallery. At the foot of the stairs is a striking large plaster cast of John Thomas's statue of Lady Godiva. The art gallery has a collection of representative Italian and Dutch old masters and temporary exhibitions are held. Some of the picture collection may now be seen in the public rooms of the Archbishop's Palace.

Museum of Kent Life, Lock Lane, Sandling, Maidstone ME14 3AU. Telephone: 01622 763936.
Open April to October, daily.

This award-winning working museum allows hands-on experience in all aspects of Kent farming, including hopping, orchards, farm animals and transport. There is a spe-

cial exhibition on *The Darling Buds of May*, which was written in Kent. Themed events are held throughout the year.

Tyrwhitt-Drake Museum of Carriages, Old Palace Stable, Maidstone ME14 1LH. Telephone: 01622 754497.
Open daily.

An exciting display of carriages, some dating back over two hundred years, is housed in the former stables of the Archbishop's Palace. The collection is named after a former Mayor of Maidstone, who established it, and includes state, official and private carriages, livery and associated items. It is the best museum of its type in Britain.

Manston
RAF Manston Hurricane and Spitfire Memorial Building, RAF Manston, Ramsgate CT12 5BS. Telephone: 01843 823351, extension 6219.
Open daily.

The museum, which is located at RAF

The Tyrwhitt-Drake Museum of Carriages is in the Old Palace Stable at Maidstone.

Manston, one of two surviving RAF airfields from the Battle of Britain, consists of two purpose-built pavilions housing genuine examples of Hurricane and Spitfire aircraft. Both aircraft served in the Second World War, the Spitfire being credited with four 'kills', and have been restored to pristine condition. The museum also contains numerous displays and many cabinets filled with memorabilia from the Second World War and the history of Manston.

Margate

Old Town Hall Museum, Market Place, Margate CT9 1ER. Telephone: 01843 231213.
Open Monday to Friday; also Saturdays and Sundays in summer.

The museum explains the development of the town as one of the earliest seaside resorts. The former courtroom and police cells may also be seen.

Milton Regis

Court Hall Museum, High Street, Milton Regis, Sittingbourne. Telephone enquiries: 01795 521515.
Open: telephone for details.

The Court Hall is a fifteenth-century timber-framed building with a crown-post roof, built to accommodate the hundred court of the Royal Manor and Demesne of Milton. It contains displays and items relating to the historic development of the area.

Minster in Sheppey

Minster Abbey Gatehouse Museum, Union Road, Minster, Sheerness ME12 2HW. Telephone enquiries: 01795 661119.
Open mid July to mid September, daily; also Easter, May and Spring bank holidays.

This imaginative museum covers the history of the Isle of Sheppey and is displayed in the gatehouse of the medieval abbey. There are excellent views from the top of the gatehouse over most of the island and out to the wreck of the *Richard Montgomery*, an ammunition ship.

Orpington

Bromley Museum, The Priory, Church Hill, Orpington BR6 0HH. Telephone: 01689

873826.
Open daily.

This small museum details the history of the London Borough of Bromley, with archaeological finds and social history. There are changing temporary exhibitions.

Ramsgate

East Kent Maritime Museum, Clock House, Pier Yard, Royal Harbour, Ramsgate CT11 8LS. Telephone: 01843 587765.
Open Monday to Friday throughout the year, plus weekends in summer.

The museum contains four galleries depicting the maritime history of east Kent, relics from Goodwin Sands wrecks, navigational equipment and lifeboat memorabilia. A number of historic boats may be seen undergoing restoration.

Ramsgate Museum, Guildford Lawn, Ramsgate CT11 9AY. Telephone: 01843 593532.
Open daily, except Sundays.

This small local history collection shows the development of Ramsgate as a seaside resort.

Rochester

Charles Dickens Centre, Eastgate House, Rochester ME1 1EW. Telephone: 01634 844176.
Open daily.

This is one of the best museums in the county, devoted to Dickens's works and in particular to the city of Rochester, where many of his books are set. Montages, audio-visual displays and exhibitions bring his work to life and visitors may see his Swiss chalet in the gardens behind the museum.

Guildhall Museum, High Street, Rochester ME1 1PY. Telephone: 01634 848717.
Open daily.

This museum of civic, commercial and maritime interest is exceptionally well displayed. The collections include archaeology, naval history and weapons. Also on view is the impressive council chamber. The former River Conservancy offices adjoining have been adapted to take the extensive collection

The Museum of Kent Life, Cobtree, has oast houses and a hop garden.

of nineteenth- and early twentieth-century objects, displayed in complete room settings. There is also a display on the history of local theatres. An exciting section is devoted to life on the prisoner-of-war ships on the Thames and Medway estuaries in the eighteenth and nineteenth centuries.

The Poor Travellers' House, 97 High Street, Rochester ME1 1LX. Telephone: 01634 845609.
Open March to October, Tuesday to Saturday.

This delightful almshouse contains a small museum relating to Richard Watt's Charity, which was founded in 1579. At the rear of the building can be seen the six bedrooms which provided free accommodation for six poor travellers, 'be they noe commen rogues or proctors', from the sixteenth century until the 1940s.

Rolvenden

Booth Historic Vehicle Collection, 63-67 High Street, Rolvenden TN17 4LP. Tele-

phone: 01580 241234.
Open daily except Sundays.

This unusual collection of vehicles includes a 1929 Morris van, motorcycles and Morgan three-wheelers. There is much motoring memorabilia including model and toy cars.

St Margaret's Bay

The Bay Museum, Beach Road, St Margaret's Bay CT15 6DZ. Telephone: 01304 852764.
Open May to September, daily except Mondays and Tuesdays.

Maritime and local history is displayed in this small but fascinating museum, where a video of the local area may be viewed.

Sandwich

Precinct Toy Collection, 38 Harnet Street, Sandwich CT13 9ES. Telephone: 01304 621114.
Open: weekend before Easter to end of September, daily; limited weekend opening in winter.

This is a lifetime's collection of toys, fur-

Smallhythe Place was the home of the actress Ellen Terry.

nished dolls' houses, Noah's arks and miniature pieces. It is suitable for wheelchairs and dogs are permitted.

Sandwich Museum, Guildhall, Cattle Market, Sandwich CT13 9AE. Telephone: 01304 617197.
Open regularly throughout the year; telephone for details.
A small but interesting display of objects relating to the history of Sandwich and further afield is housed in the Guildhall. There is access for wheelchairs.

White Mill Folk Museum, White Mill, Ash Road, Sandwich CT13 9JB (see page 99).

Sevenoaks

Sevenoaks Museum, Buckhurst Lane, Sevenoaks TN13 1LQ. Telephone: 01732 452384.
Open daily except Sundays.
This small exhibition tells the history of Sevenoaks and the surrounding area from prehistoric times to the present day, with good displays on local trades.

Sittingbourne

Dolphin Sailing Barge Museum, Crown Quay Lane, Sittingbourne ME10 3SN. Telephone: 01795 423215.
Open Easter to end of October, Sundays and bank holidays.
This small museum is housed in a former barge repair yard, the only one left in Great Britain. It consists of a shipwright's shop, a sail loft, a forge, a barge yard and basin. On display are many relics of barging days including photographs and artefacts. A section is devoted to the brickmaking industry. The famous sailing barge *Cambria* is undergoing restoration in the basin and other barges are in for repair.

Staplehurst

Brattle Farm Museum, Five Oak Lane, Staplehurst TN12 0HE. Telephone: 01580 891222.
Open Easter to October, Sundays and bank holidays.
This country museum on a working farm displays agricultural tools and skills from the past two hundred years. There is a collection of vintage cars, a pair of working oxen and much more.

Tenterden

Tenterden and District Museum, Station Road, Tenterden TN30 6HN. Telephone: 01580 764310.
Open: March, weekends only; April to October, daily except Fridays.
This museum charts the history of the town and surrounding villages. As a limb of the Cinque Ports the town has developed differently from other Wealden towns and this is reflected in its regalia, seals, weights and measures.

Tunbridge Wells

A Day at the Wells, The Pantiles, Tunbridge Wells TN2 5QJ. Telephone: 01892 546545.
Open daily.
A personal stereo tour of life in the town in 1740 is supplemented by montages and displays. The sounds, sights and smells may not be to present-day taste but they accurately reflect life under the then Master of Ceremonies, Beau Nash. A visit here is recommended as an introduction to Tunbridge Wells before starting to explore the town.

Tunbridge Wells Museum and Art Gallery, Civic Centre, Mount Pleasant, Tunbridge Wells TN1 1JN. Telephone: 01892 526121 or 547221.
Open daily except Sundays.
The collections on permanent display cover local archaeological finds, dolls, games, toys, domestic and agricultural bygones and the local iron industry. The history of the town is illustrated in prints and drawings and there is a natural history room. A display of Tunbridge ware, that wonderful and much sought-after tourist souvenir of the nineteenth century, shows a wide variety of these inlaid wooden artefacts. The art gallery has frequently changing exhibitions of work by local artists and craftspeople, touring shows from major British galleries and works from the museum's reserve collections.

Westerham

Quebec House, Westerham TN16 1TD. See page 76.

Whitstable

Whitstable Museum and Gallery, Oxford Street, Whitstable CT5 1DB. Telephone: 01227 276998.
Open daily except Wednesdays and Sundays.

This fascinating and growing collection relating to the development of this coastal town has special features on oyster fishing, diving and shipping. Town life in Victorian Whitstable is also very well represented and is a major resource for local schools. There is a noted collection of ship pictures and a gallery for changing art exhibitions.

Whitstable Oyster and Fishery Museum, East Quay, The Harbour, Whitstable CT5 1AB. Telephone: 01227 272003.
Open April to October, daily except Wednesdays.

This museum, housed in the original buildings of the Seasalter and Ham Oyster Fishery Company, tells the fascinating story of Kent's traditional oyster and fishing industry with unique artefacts, memorabilia and photographs. Amusing displays include 'hands-on' pools, a beachcomber garden and collections of fossils and shells. Local oysters and clams are on sale.

The statue of Sir Winston Churchill in Westerham is a reminder of his forty years residence at Chartwell nearby.

Right: *Herne Windmill was built in 1789 and is once again in working order.*

Below: *Sarre Windmill near Birchington is fully restored and produces wholemeal flour for sale to visitors.*

9
Watermills and windmills

All over the county the practice of building paths and walls with old millstones shows that there have been many working mills in the area. Some were water-powered, although the majority were powered by the wind. They were concentrated in the north and east of the county, where most land was under the plough in the eighteenth and nineteenth centuries. During the mid nineteenth century the establishment of mechanised mills near town centres led to the decline of small country mills and their subsequent loss from the landscape. Today there are few survivors in comparison to the two hundred or so that stood in the 1830s. Luckily, those that have survived are often well maintained, in no small part a result of the generosity of Kent County Council and the enthusiastic work done by local volunteers. Information about many of the mills in the county may be obtained from the Kent Mills Group (telephone: 01797 366020).

Chart Gunpowder Mill, Westbrook Walk, Faversham (OS 178: TR 008612). Telephone: 01795 534542.

This unusual and unique collection of buildings forms the oldest gunpowder mill of its kind in the world. Gunpowder mills were first established here in 1560 and closed in 1934, after which much of the site was demolished. Luckily one mill survived and it was saved by the town and the Faversham Society, which started restoration in 1967. It is nearly complete and open to the public. Gunpowder was produced here for both Nelson and Wellington and without it the history of England could have been very different.

Chillenden Windmill, Chillenden (OS 179: TR 269543). Telephone: 01304 840646.

Many people think that this is the best small windmill in Kent. It is a post mill, built around a central post that allows the whole structure to be turned into the wind. Situated in a large open field, it is a notable local landmark. It was built in 1868 to grind both corn and cattle feed and was last used commercially in 1949. It is well maintained and the key may be obtained locally.

Crabble Corn Mill, Lower Road, River, Dover CT17 0UY (OS 179: TR 297432). Telephone: 01304 823292.

Built in 1812 to provide flour for soldiers awaiting the threatened French invasion, this impressive six-storey mill ceased working in the 1890s. It was later restored and since 1972 the water-powered machinery has been in working order, producing stone-ground wholemeal flour. Visitors can follow the route of the grain as it is processed and the flour is sold in the shop.

Chart Gunpowder Mill at Faversham is the oldest of its kind in the world.

Cranbrook Union Windmill, Cranbrook (OS 188: TQ 779359). Telephone: 01580 712256.

This mill is in the centre of Cranbrook and is called Union Mill because when the builder became bankrupt it was run by a 'union' of his creditors! It dates from 1814 and is the best surviving smock mill in England. Built on a tall black-tarred base, its white-painted smock dominates the town centre to a much greater extent than the parish church.

Draper's Mill, Margate (OS 179: TR 363700). Telephone: 01843 291696.

Draper's Mill is an excellent example of how a windmill can be restored. It was derelict until the formation of a trust in 1965. With help this black smock mill was restored and the sails may now often be seen turning in the summer.

Herne Windmill, Mill Lane, Herne (OS 179: TR 185665). Telephone: 01227 361326.

This lovely old smock mill mounted on a two-storey brick base was built in 1789. It ceased using wind power in 1952 and for some time was powered by electricity but now it has been restored and is once more powered by the wind.

Hythe Watermill, Hythe (OS 179 and 189: TR 167350). Telephone: 01303 265032.
Open on National Mills Day and by appointment.

This weatherboarded mill was in existence in 1685, rebuilt in its present form in 1773 and continued to work until 1932. Its 21 foot (6.4 metre) waterwheel has been restored. The mill stands in extensive gardens.

Meopham Windmill, Meopham Green, Gravesend DA13 0QA (OS 177: TQ 639652). Telephone: 01474 812110.

This delightful mill stands on the main road near Meopham Green. It dates from 1801. Like many smock mills in Kent it is painted black with white sweeps. The ground floor is now a parish room, whilst the upper floors have been restored to their original appearance. An unusual and unexplained feature of the mill is that it is hexagonal in shape rather than octagonal.

Sarre Windmill, Canterbury Road, Sarre, Birchington CT7 0TU (OS 179: TR 259651). Telephone: 01843 847573.

Meopham Windmill overlooks the famous cricket ground at Meopham.

Built in 1820, this smock mill is now fully restored and the sight of its sails turning as one drives across the wide open fields is majestic. The mill produces wholemeal flour, and other visitor attractions have been established to make it a worthwhile stop between Canterbury and the Isle of Thanet.

Stelling Minnis Windmill, Stelling Minnis (OS 179: TR 146465). Telephone: 01227 709635.
Open on summer Sunday afternoons.
Built in 1866 at the peak of nineteenth-century flour production, this mill had an engine added in 1923 to aid production, the sweeps being out of service until 1935. Owned by Kent County Council, it is maintained internally by the Kent Mills Group and grinds occasionally.

Stocks Mill, Wittersham (OS 189: TQ 913273). Telephone: 01797 270537.
This post mill was built in 1781 and restored by the county council in 1980, but not to working order. It contains an exhibition of local bygones, photographs etc and a gift shop.

Swanton Watermill, Mersham, Ashford (OS 179 and 189: TR 038388). Telephone: 01233 720223.
This seventeenth-century watermill won a heritage award for its restoration in 1975. It

can be seen in full working order and stone-ground flour is on sale. There is a museum display and an extensive garden.

White Mill, Ash Road, Sandwich CT13 9JB (OS 179: TR 322586). Telephone: 01304 612076.
This smock mill is the only one to survive in a town that once had several. It dates from the late eighteenth and early nineteenth centuries and was restored by Vincent Pargeter, one of today's leading craftsmen. It now houses a folk museum.

Willesborough Windmill, Willesborough, Ashford (OS 179 and 189: TR 032422). Telephone: 01304 612076.
This working smock mill is maintained by a trust. Guided tours of the mill are given and visitors are able to see the miller's cottage and restored barn, the former furnished as it would have been before 1939.

Woodchurch Windmill, Woodchurch (OS 189: TQ 943353). Telephone: 01233 860043.
During the late 1970s and early 1980s this early nineteenth-century smock mill was rescued from complete dereliction and restored to working order and to house an exhibition of photographs. Until the 1930s a second mill stood nearby and together they were known as the 'Woodchurch twins'.

10
Other places to visit

Badsell Park Farm, Crittenden Road, Matfield, Tonbridge TN12 7EW. Telephone: 01892 832549.
Open daily.

This fruit and arable farm, run by a charity, is a centre for education, aimed especially at children from inner cities. There is much to see for all visitors, including farm and domestic animals, nature displays and country walks.

Battle of Britain Memorial, New Dover Road, Capel-le-Ferne, Folkestone CT18 7JN. Telephone: 01303 249292 or 276697.
Open: accessible at all times (car park open 1st April to 11th November).

This is the National Memorial to those who flew in the Battle of Britain. A stone figure of a pilot in contemplative mood, overlooking the Channel, serves as a central figure for the three-bladed propeller within the grassed arena. This memorial stands as a permanent tribute to the bravery and sacrifice of all those who served Great Britain so unselfishly in her hour of need.

Brambles English Wildlife and Rare Breeds, Herne Common, Canterbury. Telephone: 01227 712379.
Open Easter to Christmas, daily.

This very popular wildlife park enables the visitor to see wild animals at close quarters and to support the rescue work carried out by the centre. Sick and injured animals are brought in and cared for in enclosures set in the lovely woodland. There is a children's corner, a picnic area and a toad garden!

Brogdale Orchards, Brogdale Road, Faversham ME13 8XZ. Telephone: 01795 535286.
Open daily.

The National Fruit Collection, established in 30 acres (12 hectares) of managed orchard, displays over four thousand varieties of fruit trees and plants. Guided tours are available during the summer, and the site is open all year round, with experts on hand to give advice to fruit growers.

The Butterfly Centre, Macfarlanes Garden Centre, on A260, Swingfield, near Dover CT15 7HX. Telephone: 01303 844244.
Open April to early October, daily except Easter Day.

A spacious tropical greenhouse contains a large collection of free-flying butterflies from all over the world. There is an educational display.

Chislehurst Caves, Old Hill, Chislehurst BR7 5NB. Telephone: 0181-467 3264.
Open Wednesday to Sunday; daily in school holidays.

Chislehurst Caves became well-known following their use as air-raid shelters in the Second World War, when up to fifteen thousand Londoners came here by train each night. The caves were formed by the mining of chalk for building and agriculture. The main passages are only two hundred years old, but some parts of the complex may be much older. Although much is made of their possible prehistoric origins, the main attraction of the caves is their wartime use and a guided tour is guaranteed to thrill.

Cobham Manor Riding Centre, Water Lane, Thurnham, Maidstone ME14 3LU. Telephone: 01622 738497.

This is the leading equestrian centre in the county, with circular walks (leaflets available), rides, cycle routes and a network of bridleways starting here. There is a tack shop.

David Evans World of Silk, Bourne Industrial Estate, Bourne Road, Crayford DA1 4BP. Telephone: 01322 559401.
Open daily except Sundays and bank holi-

days. Guided tours should be pre-booked.

Few factory tours are available in Kent but David Evans offers tours of the silk mills, with displays on how silk and other materials are finished. There is an excellent small museum which illustrates the history of silk and shows the different tools used to produce particular effects. There is a good silk factory shop.

Dreamland Theme Park, Marine Terrace, Margate CT9 1XL. Telephone: 01843 227011.

Open daily in the summer.

Kent's oldest theme park, Dreamland has been popular with holidaymakers for sixty years. Some of the original rides survive, but the emphasis is on the latest white-knuckle attractions.

Dungeness Power Station, Dungeness, Romney Marsh TN29 9PP. Telephone: 01797 321815.

Open daily, except winter Saturdays; pre-booking recommended.

An unusual day out may be had seeing how electricity is made from nuclear power. There is an excellent visitor centre with interactive displays. A guided tour then takes in the turbine hall and control room. At the end of the tour there is the opportunity to visit the nature trail laid out in the starkly beautiful landscape of this unique part of Kent.

Dunrobin Stud Farm, Dunes Road, Greatstone, New Romney. Telephone: 01797 363335.

Open: telephone for details.

This is a unique collection of twenty stallions, with Shire horses and other farm animals.

Eagle Heights, Lullingstone Lane, Eynsford, Kent DA4 0JB. Telephone: 01322 866466.

Open March to November, daily; December to February, weekends only.

This bird of prey centre has flying displays and indoor demonstrations where visitors can learn about the various hawks, falcons, eagles and owls housed here.

East Kent Light Railway, Station Road, Shepherdswell, Dover. Telephone: 01304 832042.

Open regularly in summer; telephone for details.

This railway was originally built for transporting coal from the Kent mines. Following closure of the collieries, the line between Shepherdswell and Eythorne has reopened to carry passengers. Special events are held throughout the year. Attractions include a museum and a miniature railway.

The Elham Valley Railway Exhibition, Peene, Newington, Folkestone CT18 8BA. Telephone: 01303 273690.

Open April to September, weekends only.

The railway museum tells the story of the Elham Valley branch line, which ran through 16½ miles (27 km) of beautiful countryside between Folkestone and Canterbury from 1884 to 1947. There is an extensive working model of the line. A new exhibit is a fully working scenic model of the English terminal of the Channel Tunnel, modelled on the real terminal at neighbouring Cheriton.

Farming World, Nash Court, Boughton, Faversham ME13 9SW. Telephone: 01227 751144.

Open March to October daily; weekends only in winter.

A museum and trail have been established at this 'hands-on' farm, where the visitor is encouraged to get to know the animals and techniques of a working farm. There are 'pick-your-own' fields in season and special themed events throughout the year.

Great Stour Brewery and Museum, Stour Street, Canterbury. Telephone: 01227 763579.

Open: telephone for details.

This unusual brewery produces beer at just 40p per pint! These prices are possible because the brewery provides the equipment and members of the public brew their own beer in batches of 100 pints, which means that it is free of customs and excise duty! Computer-aided design allows customers to design their own labels, creating a unique product. Tours are available to see the coppers, and a shop stocks many real ales from across Britain.

Headcorn Flower Centre and Vineyard, Grigg Lane, Headcorn, Ashford TN27 9LX. Telephone: 01622 890250.
Open daily for self-guided tours; guided tours available in summer.

Over five million sprays of flowers are produced each year in the 7 acres (2.8 hectares) of flower houses, which may be visited. There is particular emphasis on chrysanthemums and lilies. Part of the site is given over to a vineyard and the greenhouse tour is suitable for the disabled.

The Hop Shop, Castle Farm, Shoreham, Sevenoaks TN14 7UB. Telephone: 01959 523219.
Open Monday to Friday afternoons and Saturdays.

This fascinating farm shop is housed in a lovely old barn whose beams are hung with hops. A flower arranger's paradise, devoted to dried flowers, it is also of interest to casual visitors, who will be amazed at the colourful displays. Regular courses are held.

Howletts Wild Animal Park, Bekesbourne Lane, Bekesbourne, Canterbury CT4 5EL. Telephone: 01227 721286.
Open daily.

Howletts, owned by John Aspinall, is set in 70 acres (28 hectares) of beautiful ancient parkland and is home to the largest captive gorilla breeding group in the world. It is the aim of the park to breed endangered species and reintroduce them to protected areas in the wild. Other endangered species to be seen at the park are African elephants, Siberian and Indian tigers, snow leopards, wolves, tapirs and many unusual primates.

Iden Croft Herbs, Frittenden Road, Staplehurst TN12 0DH. Telephone: 01580 891432.
Open daily except winter Sundays.

Thousands of herbs, including many rare varieties, set in charming gardens, may be viewed from a network of paths. The collection includes the National Collections of both Mint and Origanum. There is a programme of special events and many plants are for sale.

Kent & East Sussex Railway, Tenterden Town Station, Tenterden TN30 6HE. Telephone: 01580 765155.
Open April to October, weekends, bank holidays and school holidays; more often in summer; telephone for timetable details.

Passengers on this charming rural railway can savour the characteristic sights and sounds of steam as they travel through 7 miles (11 km) of attractive countryside from Tenterden to the East Sussex village of Northiam. One payment allows travel all day aboard the magnificent Victorian train or in carriages from the 1930s and 1950s. Many trains have buffet cars and facilities for the disabled.

Margate Caves, 1 Northdown Road, Cliftonville, Margate CT9 2RN. Telephone: 01843 220139.
Open Easter to October, daily.

These caves were dug in the seventeenth century to supply chalk for agricultural purposes. Although they are near the sea they never connected to the beach. The main workings are light and airy, but the later additions, including what may be a small malt kiln, are claustrophobic. There are extensive wall paintings dating from the late eighteenth century when the local parson connected the caves to his cellars to provide more storage space. They depict local hunting scenes and Napoleonic soldiers. During the Second World War they were used as air-raid shelters.

Martello Tower Visitors' Centre, Wear Bay Road, Folkestone. Telephone: 01303 850388.
Open: June to September, daily; October to December, weekends only.

This visitors' centre is housed in one of the martello towers built between 1803 and 1805. It contains displays relating to the natural history of Folkestone Warren and to the local history of this clifftop area.

Nepicar Farm, Wrotham Heath. Telephone: 01732 883040.
Open March to October, daily.

This working farm, set close to the M26, contains rare breeds and a large flock of milking sheep. The cheesemaking unit, the only place in Kent where farmhouse cheese is made from sheep's milk, may be visited, and it is possible to purchase the famous Cecilia cheese matured on beds of Kentish hops. There is a woodland walk and farm trail. The farm is the site of one of the oldest and largest boot fairs in England.

Old Brook Pumping Station, Solomons Road, The Brook, Chatham ME4 4LA. Telephone: 01634 842059.
Open Tuesday evenings and Saturday mornings (telephone to confirm).
Until 1980 this pumping station was part of Chatham's drainage system. It is now run by the Medway Industrial Archaeology Group as a small living museum, and the two Campbell oil engines are usually run when the station is open to the public.

Old Dungeness Lighthouse, Dungeness, Romney Marsh. Telephone: 01679 321300.
Open: Easter to September, daily; October, weekends only.
The lighthouse was built in the early twentieth century but is now redundant. The coast at Dungeness grows by several feet each year,

and a better-placed lighthouse was built in 1960. From the top, reached by climbing 167 steps, there are excellent views over the expanses of shingle and the nuclear power station.

Paddle Steamer *Kingswear Castle*, Historic Dockyard, Chatham ME4 4TQ. Telephone: 01634 827648.
Open: telephone for timetable of sailings.
A unique part of Britain's maritime heritage, the award-winning coal-fired paddle steamer *Kingswear Castle* provides morning, afternoon, evening and full-day excursions from the Chatham Historic Dockyard and Rochester Pier. Travellers sail back into history aboard a real steamship, see the steam engine turning the paddles and watch the scenery glide by.

Parsonage Farm Rural Heritage Centre, North Elham, near Canterbury CT4 6UY. Telephone: 01303 840766.
Open Easter to September, daily except Mondays.
On this family farm visitors can see tradional and rare breeds of farm animals, in-

The new Dungeness Lighthouse was built in 1960. The old lighthouse which it superseded still stands and is open to the public.

cluding many breeds of sheep. Displays show the history of the farm and of wool and cereal production.

Philippine Village Craft Centre, Brookland, Romney Marsh. Telephone: 01797 344616.
Open: Easter to end of May, weekends only; end of May to end of September, daily.
The craft centre is an exotic place to come across in the bleak marshland landscape. Visitors may purchase furniture, jewellery, clothing and shells from the 'pearl of the Orient'.

Port Lympne Wild Animal Park, Mansion and Gardens, Lympne, near Hythe CT21 4PD. Telephone: 01303 264647.
Open daily.
The historic mansion was built in 1913 by Sir Herbert Baker for Sir Philip Sassoon MP amongst 15 acres (6 hectares) of landscaped gardens commanding wonderful views over Romney Marsh. John Aspinall has restored the house and turned the park over to rare breeds and endangered species. A new pavilion and outdoor enclosure for gorillas proves very popular with visitors and extensive walks may be taken through the 300 acres (121 hectares) of paddocks and woods.

Ramsgate Model Village, West Cliff, Ramsgate. Telephone: 01843 592543.
Open Easter to end of October, daily.
This beautifully maintained model village is missed by many who choose to stay by the harbour. It represents all aspects of English life.

Romney Hythe & Dymchurch Railway, New Romney Station, New Romney TN28 8PL. Telephone: 01797 362353.
Open April to September, daily; March and October, weekends only.
The railway comprises 14 miles (23 km) of track joining Hythe and Dungeness via Dymchurch and New Romney. The gauge is 15 inches (381 mm). Trains run a regular service and in term time there is a school special, making this the smallest railway in the world to run scheduled services. Wide areas of Romney Marsh can be appreciated from the carriages. There are eleven steam locomotives and one diesel, all built to one-third of full size. The Toy and Model Museum at New Romney station features one of the largest model railways in Britain.

The Royal Military Canal
The Royal Military Canal was built on the orders of William Pitt as a defence against a French invasion, a second line of resistance for use if the martello towers were to fall. The plan was then to flood Romney Marsh, cutting off the invaders from their supply source. The canal runs for over 23 miles (37 km) along the northern edge of the marsh and was defended by cannon and small forts that could be reached from inland behind a tall earth bank. Work started in 1803 after war had been declared for the second time in ten years but even before the canal was finished it was out of date. Today it is used mainly by fishermen. Fine stretches may be seen wherever roads lead off the marsh, particularly at Appledore, Warehorne and Bilsington. In alternate years a Venetian fete is held on the canal at Hythe – an exotic use for an exotic idea!

Shell Grotto, Grotto Hill, Margate CT9 2BU. Telephone: 01843 220008.
Open Easter to October, daily.
The grotto was first opened to the public in 1837. It is an underground chamber, the walls and ceilings of which are entirely covered with sea shells. Many people believe it is two thousand years old although it may actually have been built in the late eighteenth century. The patterns formed by the shells represent flowers, stars and phallic symbols. Most of the shells have lost their original colouring, but it is a remarkable place, almost unexpected in the built-up area of this part of Margate.

Sittingbourne & Kemsley Light Railway, The Wall, Milton Regis, Sittingbourne. Telephone: 01622 755313.
Open on Sundays from Easter to mid October, plus Wednesdays and Saturdays in August and all bank holidays. Telephone for details.
This was originally an industrial narrow-gauge line used to take the products of the

paper mills at Sittingbourne and Kemsley to the docks. The gauge is 2 feet 6 inches (762 mm). There are good views to be had over the marshes and industrial landscape.

South of England Rare Breeds Centre, Woodchurch, Ashford TN26 3RJ. Telephone: 01233 861493.
Open daily except winter Mondays.

This interesting collection contains over five hundred farm animals of historic breeds, many of which may be touched and handled. In the summer farm rides are often available and there is a comprehensive programme of events throughout the year. The farm is a very special place as it offers those with mental disabilities the chance of work and training at this busy tourist attraction.

South Foreland Lighthouse, St Margaret's Bay. Telephone: 01304 202756. National Trust.
Open April to October, weekends only.

Charles I granted permission for the building here in 1643 of high and low lighthouses, lit with open fires. They were rebuilt in 1843 and 1846, but the lower light was put out as the cliff eroded. In 1859 South Foreland was the first lighthouse in the world to use electricity and in 1899 Marconi experimented with wireless telegraphy, putting the lighthouse in communication with the Goodwins lightship.

Theatre Royal, 102 High Street, Chatham. Telephone: 01634 831028.
Open daily except Sundays.

The Theatre Royal is the most impressive building in Chatham High Street. Built in 1899, it was the largest theatre in Kent. After closure in the 1950s it was subdivided and converted into shops and storehouses. In 1995 it was purchased by a charitable trust, which is restoring it to its former glory. Regular guided tours of the building, where restoration work may be seen in progress, are given and interest in the building and its social and architectural history is encouraged.

Tyland Barn, Sandling, Maidstone. Telephone: 01622 662012.
Open February to December, daily except Mondays.

This seventeenth-century barn contains a major exhibition centre displaying Kent's heritage of wildlife and conservation, with events, walks and tours. There is a natural habitat garden where wildlife may be studied at first hand.

Vineyards in Kent

Wine has been produced in the county since Roman times and there are a number of vineyards where visitors can walk around and learn how wine is made. Often the wine may be tasted and purchased on site.

Ash Coombe Vineyard, Coombe Lane, Ash, Canterbury. Telephone: 01304 813396.

Biddenden Vineyards, Little Whatmans, Biddenden. Telephone: 01580 291726.

Elham Valley Vineyards, Breach, Barham, Canterbury. Telephone: 01227 831266.

Headcorn Flower Centre Vineyard, Grigg Lane, Headcorn, Ashford TN27 9LX. Telephone: 01622 890250. See also page 102.

Kent Garden Vineyard, Yew Tree House, Upper Street, Leeds. Telephone: 01622 861638.

Lamberhurst Vineyard, Ridge Farm, Lamberhurst. Telephone: 01892 890844.

Penshurst Vineyard, Grove Road, Penshurst. Telephone: 01892 870255.

St Nicholas Vineyard, Moat Farm, Ash. Telephone: 01304 812670.

Staple Vineyards, Church Farm, Staple. Telephone: 01304 812571.

Tenterden Vineyards, Spots Farm, Tenterden. Telephone: 01580 63033.

Wingham Bird Park, Wingham, Canterbury CT3 1JL. Telephone: 01227 720836.
Open daily.

This interesting bird park contains owls, parrots and many species of waterfowl. It stands within 15 acres (6 hectares) of countryside and includes a walk-through aviary, pet village and adventure playground. The emphasis is on environmentally friendly techniques and most of the park is built of recycled materials.

11
Men and women of Kent

Kent has had many famous people associated with it. Its position close to the continent has meant that travellers have been passing through for centuries. Some have stayed – or at least used the county as a base from which easy access to both capital and continent might be gained.

The earliest figures were religious men and women who founded monastic houses in the county during the seventh and eighth centuries. One of the most interesting was **St Mildred**, whose mother, Domneva, founded Minster Abbey on the Isle of Thanet. Mildred was sent to France to be educated in an abbey there, but a possessive abbess threw her into an oven in a fit of temper. However, a miracle followed and Mildred survived to follow her mother as abbess at Minster (see page 66). She was buried there and the place of her shrine is known, although in the eleventh century her remains were reinterred at St Augustine's Abbey in Canterbury. The parish church at Tenterden is one of those in the county that is dedicated to her.

In the tenth century **St Dunstan** was Archbishop of Canterbury. He ordered that church bells should be rung to announce the times of service, and he once pinched the Devil's nose with a pair of tongs! Until 1170 Dunstan was England's favourite saint, but in that year **Thomas à Becket** was murdered at Canterbury and took Dunstan's place in people's affections. Becket's place of martyrdom has been marked by a modern altar and cross and, although his shrine has long gone, this small enclosure of floor is for many people the destination of their pilgrimage.

Charles Dickens accepted Kent as his home. When Charles was five his father took work at Chatham Dockyard and Dickens's long association with the county began. His first home was in Ordnance Terrace opposite Chatham railway station. As a boy he would often walk in the countryside and once remarked to his father that he would like to live in a particular house. Some thirty years later, having become a successful journalist, he was able to buy the house, Gad's Hill (see page 71), where he lived until his death in 1870. The whole area of north and east Kent provided him with inspiration. The opening scenes of *Great Expectations* are set in the graveyard at Cooling, where one can still see Pip's Graves and the distant Thames, where the prison hulks were moored. At Cobham the Leather Bottle Inn was made famous in *The Pickwick Papers*, whilst Cobtree Manor near Maidstone was the original of Dingley Dell in the same book. On the coast, Broadstairs (pages 12 and 79) influenced his writings but it was Rochester (pages 28, 67 and 91) that is to be found in most of his books, thinly disguised. In *The Mystery of Edwin Drood* it is called Cloisterham and described in the minutest detail. Although tradition says that Dickens wished to be buried in Rochester he was eventually buried in Westminster Abbey, although there is a memorial to him in Rochester Cathedral.

An earlier author and playwright associated with the county was **Christopher Marlowe**. Born in Canterbury in 1564, he became a scholar at the King's School in the city when he was about fourteen. At the age of seventeen he went to Cambridge and quickly became accepted as a poet under the patronage of Sir Thomas Walsingham. In 1593 he was murdered in a pub fight at Deptford, at the age of just twenty-nine. During his lifetime he was known as the 'father of English blank verse'.

In 1768 **William Shipley**, an artist, inventor and founder of the Royal Society of Arts, moved to Maidstone. He was an ingenious gentleman who invented a 'floating light' for the benefit of those who had fallen overboard from ships and he also recommended the insertion of tin foil in one's shoes to keep them warm! Knightrider House, his home in Maidstone, stands near All Saints' church, where he was buried in 1803. His monument in the north-west corner of the churchyard was restored in 1977 by the Royal Society of Arts.

One of the best-loved actresses of the twentieth century, **Dame Sybil Thorndike**, lived in Kent during her early years. Her father, a clergyman, was appointed a minor canon of Rochester Cathedral in 1884 when Sybil was just two. They lived in Minor Canon Row (see page 29) but when she was ten her family moved to another house in the city. Whilst living in Rochester she took part in her first plays. In 1904 she went on her first tour of America. Her father was made Vicar of Aylesford in the same year and it was in Aylesford church that she was married in 1908. Her parents are buried in the churchyard there, although they had moved away from the area in 1909. Sybil continued to visit the area until her death in 1976.

One of the most famous queens of England, **Anne Boleyn**, spent her early years at Hever Castle (see page 55). Her father was a prominent member of Henry VIII's household and Anne had caught the King's eye. He visited her often at Hever and when he heard that she was ill he sent his own physician to tend her. Yet their courting was troublesome. She refused to be his mistress and was determined to become his queen or nothing. She was married to Henry in January 1533, and Henry's marriage to Catherine of Aragon was dissolved in May. By 1536 Anne had fallen from favour and was beheaded in the Tower of London. Her parents were shunned by the court and died a few years later, at which time Henry took possession of Hever and gave it to his new queen, Anne of Cleves.

William Willett, who conceived the idea of daylight saving (British Summer Time), lived in Kent and is buried in the churchyard of St Nicholas, Chislehurst. In nearby Petts Wood is a memorial to him, taking the form of a sundial which shows only British Summer Time.

Henry Fox, first **Lord Holland**, used Kent as a retreat in the middle of the eighteenth century. As Paymaster General to the Forces he had been accused on more than one occasion of misusing public money. He thought that by purchasing a stretch of lonely coastline between Margate and Broadstairs he could get away from his critics and spend his time in constructive enjoyment. As he said, 'the truth is, I divert myself'. Most of his diversions took the form of follies. Holland House itself was a magnificent Italianate villa full of marbles and other classical decorations. In the grounds Lord Holland built temples, a castle, a convent and numerous tow-

'Pip's Graves' can be visited in Cooling churchyard, a reminder of Dickens's 'Great Expectations'.

ers. The remains of his 'Bede House' are now incorporated into the Captain Digby public house. This is named after Bob Digby, a retired seaman who was employed here to served Lord Holland's visitors with a stiff drink on the clifftop! His towers were built for many reasons but the two largest commemorated specific men. One was Robert Whitfield, from whom he had purchased the estate, and the other was Robert Harley, who as Lord Mayor of London had been the only man to support Lord Holland when an inquiry into the Paymaster's accounts seemed certain. Today Holland House is divided into apartments, but some follies remain and can be appreciated from the clifftop walk that runs around this delightful piece of coast.

The nineteenth century was a period of great religious fervour. Throughout Kent the rapidly expanding population in the industrial towns found release in small dissenting congregations. One of the strangest and most successful was the New House of Israel. Its members followed the teachings of Joanna Southcott, an early nineteenth-century mystic. Their Kent headquarters was at Gillingham, where in 1863 their leader died, leaving no obvious successor. Some years passed. In 1875 James Rowland White joined the army locally and started to attend the meetings of the New House of Israel. Within a few months he had convinced the congregation that he was their chosen leader. However, the national headquarters refused to recognise him and he left to form the 'New and Latter House of Israel', taking most of the congregation with him. In 1876 he was sent abroad with his regiment but he continued to run the Gillingham church by sending home regular sermons. In 1881 he was discharged from the army and changed his name to **James Jershom Jezreel**, after a biblical prophet. To join the sect one had to sell everything and give it to the church, and also to pledge a tenth of all future income. The church soon became very wealthy and Jezreel started to build a tower at the top of Canterbury Street as a meeting place for his members. It was a huge and impressive structure that stood, unfinished, until its demolition in 1961. Gradually the sect declined in numbers and today the

only reminders of Gillingham's exotic past are in local street names.

During the sixteenth century the tiny village of Aldington was the home of **Elizabeth Barton**, known throughout Britain as the 'Holy Maid of Kent'. She was born in 1506 and worked as a servant to Thomas Cobb, a steward of the Archbishop of Canterbury. She suffered poor health and at the age of nineteen developed an illness that was probably epilepsy. Lambarde, the sixteenth-century historian, made an accurate account of her illness, which was made all the more remarkable by Elizabeth's visions. Her first prophecy concerned a sickly infant who, she said, would soon die. No sooner had she said it than the child passed away! Soon afterwards she had a vision telling her to go to a little chapel at Court at Street, where she would be cured. After praying there she was cured! The Archbishop of Canterbury heard of this miracle and ordered an investigation, which showed that she was telling the truth. Elizabeth was then admitted to a convent in Canterbury. So great was her following that in 1530 Henry VIII granted her an audience. Stupidly, Elizabeth told him not to divorce Catherine of Aragon in favour of Anne Boleyn. The Archbishop of Canterbury supported her, but after his death two years later Henry ordered her to be tried and Cranmer found that her 'inspiration and ecstasies were merely juggle and deceit'. She was taken to Tyburn and hanged, becoming Kent's best-known martyr after Thomas à Becket.

Soon after Elizabeth's death, in another part of the county, **Sir Philip Sidney** was born. His father had been given Penshurst Place (see page 76) by Edward VI. After education at Shrewsbury, Philip travelled widely, his charismatic personality and intelligence bringing him many friends. On his return to England he fell out with Queen Elizabeth I by advising her against a politically motivated marriage to the Duke of Anjou. To fill his time he took to writing and produced the first critical essay and the finest love poetry of the period. In 1586, when he was thirty-two, the Queen sent him to Holland, where he was killed at the battle of Zutphen. His body was brought back to England, where he was given a hero's funeral in St Paul's Cathedral. A display at Penshurst Place charts his influence over the court and country during the sixteenth century.

Richard Barham was born in 1788 and was educated at London and Oxford. He was ordained priest and in 1813 became a curate in Ashford. After marriage he moved to Snargate on Romney Marsh, but the stipend there was insufficient to support a family and he was forced to teach in Ashford to supplement his income. One day, on his way home, he was thrown from his carriage and broke his legs. This forced him to rest for several months and he took up writing almost by chance. Although his early writings are not distinguished they gave him an opening and by the time he was appointed a canon of St Paul's Cathedral in 1821 he had a reputation as a journalist. With Fleet Street close at hand, he found additional outlets for his work and started to write *The Ingoldsby Legends*. These were an unusual mixture of fact and fiction which was to become one of the standard works of the period, comparable to *The Pickwick Papers*. Many of his experiences in Kent – the woodland around Ashford and the marshland around Snargate – were incorporated in his works. He always wrote under the pen-name of Thomas Ingoldsby. His death in 1845 was a result of bronchitis that had plagued him since his days on the unhealthy Romney Marsh.

Of the many artists who have been associated with Kent, one of the saddest was **Richard Dadd**. He was born in 1817 in Chatham, where his father was a chemist. In 1834 the family moved to London, where his father took up water gilding. This brought the young Richard into artistic circles and he started to study at the Royal Academy. It was there that he met Sir Thomas Philips, who asked Richard to accompany him on a trip to the Middle East as an illustrator. On this journey Richard became ill and mentally unstable. Whether it was the heat or the cultural shock that caused this is not known, but he returned to London, where his father cared for him. His father, who believed there was nothing wrong with Richard, took him for a special treat to Cobham Park, which had been a favourite childhood haunt. After lunch at the village inn they strolled through the park, where Richard hacked his father to death. In a case that attracted international interest he was found insane and spent the last forty-three years of his life in a mental institution. It was during this period that he was most prolific, painting scenes from his eastern tours and fantasies. Today he is remembered as one of the greatest artists of the nineteenth century.

Another nineteenth-century artist was **William Morris**, who lived in Red House at Upton just outside Bexleyheath for six years. A romance in red brick, it was designed for him by his friend Philip Webb. He moved here in 1860, having just married Jane Burden, and it was intended to be a family home for them and their close friends. The house was intended to be an expression of his ambitions – to have craftsmanship and artistic talent to the fore. However, six years later, when Morris was suffering from poor health and his firm was experiencing commercial problems, he had to sell Red House and for the remaining thirty years of his life he could never bear to return. The house is open to groups by prior written appointment. Another famous member of Morris's Pre-Raphaelite Brotherhood, **Dante Gabriel Rossetti**, died in Kent at Birchington and is buried in the graveyard there.

Many other famous people have connections with Kent, including the following: **Thomas Aveling** (1824-82), steam traction engineer, buried at Hoo St Werburgh; **Sir Malcolm Campbell** (1885-1948), who broke both the land and the water speed records and is buried in St Nicholas's churchyard, Chislehurst; **Octavia Hill** (1838-1912), founder of the National Trust, buried at Crockham Hill; **Lionel Lukin** (1742-1834), inventor of the lifeboat, buried at Hythe; **E. M. Nesbit** (1858-1924), author of *The Railway Children*, buried at St Mary in the Marsh; **John Read** (died 1847), inventor of the stomach pump and round oast, buried at Horsmonden; **Graham Sutherland** (1903-80), artist, buried at Trottiscliffe; **Mary Tourtel** (1874-1948), creator of Rupert Bear, buried at St Martin's, Canterbury.

12
Tourist information centres

Centres marked with an asterisk* are open only in summer.

Ashford: 18 The Churchyard, Ashford TN23 1QG. Telephone: 01233 629165.

Bexley: Hall Place Visitor Centre, Bourne Road, Bexley DA5 1PQ. Telephone: 0181-303 9052.

Bexleyheath: Central Library, Townley Road, Bexleyheath DA6 7HJ. Telephone: 0181-303 9052.

Broadstairs: 6B High Street, Broadstairs CT10 1LH. Telephone: 01843 862242.

Canterbury: 34 St Margaret's Street, Canterbury CT1 2TG. Telephone: 01227 766567.

Cranbrook: *Vestry Hall, Stone Street, Cranbrook TN17 3HA. Telephone: 01580 712538.

Dartford: The Clocktower, Suffolk Road, Dartford DA1 1EJ. Telephone: 01322 343243.

Deal: Town Hall, High Street, Deal CT14 6BB. Telephone: 01304 369576.

Dover: Townwall Street, Dover CT16 1JR. Telephone: 01304 205108.

Faversham: Fleur de Lis Heritage Centre, 13 Preston Street, Faversham ME13 8NS. Telephone: 01795 534542.

Folkestone: Harbour Street, Folkestone CT20 1QN. Telephone: 01303 258594.

Gravesend: 10 Parrock Street, Gravesend DA12 1EL. Telephone: 01474 337600.

Herne Bay: 12 William Street, Herne Bay CT6 5EJ. Telephone: 01227 361911.

Hythe: *Prospect Road Car Park, Hythe CT21 5NH. Telephone: 01303 267799.

Maidstone: The Gatehouse, Old Palace Gardens, Maidstone ME15 6YE. Telephone: 01622 673581 or 602169.

Margate: 22 High Street, Margate CT9 1DS. Telephone: 01843 220241.

New Romney: *Light Railway Car Park, 2 Littlestone Road, New Romney TN28 8PL. Telephone: 01797 364044.

Ramsgate: 19 Harbour Street, Ramsgate CT11 8HA. Telephone: 01843 591086.

Rochester: 95 High Street, Rochester ME1 1LX. Telephone: 01634 843666.

Sandwich: *The Guildhall, Cattle Market, Sandwich CT13 9AH. Telephone: 01304 613565.

Sevenoaks: Buckhurst Lane, Sevenoaks TN13 1LQ. Telephone: 01732 450305.

Tenterden: *Town Hall, High Street, Tenterden TN30 6AN. Telephone: 01580 763572.

Tonbridge: Tonbridge Castle, Castle Street, Tonbridge TN9 1BG. Telephone: 01732 770929.

Tunbridge Wells: The Old Fish Market, The Pantiles, Tunbridge Wells TN2 5TN. Telephone: 01892 515675.

Whitstable: 7 Oxford Street, Whitstable CT5 1BB. Telephone: 01227 275482.

13
Further reading

General

Bignell, Alan. *Kent Lore*. Hale, 1983.

Bignell, Alan. *The Kent Village Book*. Countryside Books, 1986.

Brentall, Margaret. *The Cinque Ports and Romney Marsh*. John Gifford, 1972.

Guy, John. *Kent Castles*. Meresborough Books, 1980.

Major, Alan. *Who's Buried Where in Kent*. Meresborough Books, 1990.

Major, Alan. *Hidden Kent*. Countryside Books, 1994.

Mee, Arthur. *Kent*. Hodder & Stoughton, 1936.

Newman, John. *The Buildings of England: Kent* (two volumes). Penguin, 1969.

Reynolds, Kev. *The Visitor's Guide to Kent*. Moorland, 1985.

Vigar, John E. *Kent Curiosities*. Dovecote Press, 1992.

Vigar, John E. *Kent Churches*. Alan Sutton, 1995.

Selected works of fiction set in Kent

Bates, H.E. *The Darling Buds of May*.

Dickens, Charles. *Great Expectations*.

Dickens, Charles. *The Mystery of Edwin Drood*.

Dickens, Charles. *The Pickwick Papers*.

Thorndike, Russell. *Dr Syn*.

Index